WESTMAR COLLE

P9-DYP-901

Dan Ovemyer

October 1, 1986

WESTMAR COLLEGE LIBRARY

RELIGIONS
OF
CHINA

Volumes in the Religious Traditions of the World Series

Edited by H. Byron Earhart

RELIGIONS

OF

CHINA

*The World as
a Living System*

DANIEL L. OVERMYER

1817

105800

HARPER & ROW, PUBLISHERS, SAN FRANCISCO
*Cambridge, Hagerstown, New York, Philadelphia
London, Mexico City, São Paulo, Singapore, Sydney*

RELIGIONS OF CHINA: *The World as a Living System.*
Copyright © 1986 by Daniel L. Overmyer. All rights reserved.
Printed in the United States of America. No part of this book may
be used or reproduced in any manner whatsoever without written
permission except in the case of brief quotations embodied in
critical articles and reviews. For information address Harper &
Row, Publishers, Inc., 10 East 53rd Street, New York, NY
10022. Published simultaneously in Canada by Fitzhenry &
Whiteside, Limited, Toronto.

FIRST EDITION

All photos by Daniel L. Overmyer
Designed by Donna Davis

Library of Congress Cataloging in Publication Data

Overmyer, Daniel L.
   Religions of China.

   (Religious traditions of the world)
   Bibliography: p.
   1. China—Religion.   I. Title.   II. Series.
BL1802.094   1985   291'.0951   ·   85-42789
ISBN 0-06-066401-0

---

86 87 88 89 90 *MPC* 10 9 8 7 6 5 4 3 2 1

for my mother,

Bernice A. Overmyer

Contents

■

Religious Traditions of the World

O ne of human history's most fascinating aspects is the richness and variety of its religious traditions—from the earliest times to the present, in every area of the world. The ideal way to learn about all these religions would be to visit the homeland of each—to discuss the scriptures or myths with members of these traditions, explore their shrines and sacred places, view their customs and rituals. Few people have the luxury of leisure and money to take such trips, of course; nor are many prepared to make a systematic study of even those religions that are close at hand. Thus this series of books is a substitute for an around-the-world trip to many different religious traditions: it is an armchair pilgrimage through a number of traditions both distant and different from one another, as well as some situated close to one another in time, space, and religious commitment.

Individual volumes in this series focus on one or more religions, emphasizing the distinctiveness of each tradition while considering it within a comparative context. What links the volumes as a series is a shared concern for religious traditions and a common format for discussing them. Generally, each volume will explore the history of a tradition, interpret it as a unified set of religious beliefs and practices, and give examples of religious careers and typical practices. Individual volumes are self-contained treatments and can be taken up in any sequence. They are introductory, providing interested readers with an overall interpretation of religious traditions without presupposing prior knowledge.

The author of each book combines special knowledge of a religious tradition with considerable experience in teaching and communicating an interpretation of that tradition. This special knowledge includes familiarity with various languages, investigation of religious texts and historical development, and direct contact with the peoples and practices under study. The authors have refined their special knowledge through many years of teaching and writing to frame a general interpretation of the tradition that is responsible to the best-known facts and is readily available to the interested reader.

Let me join with the authors of the series in wishing you an enjoyable and profitable experience in learning about religious traditions of the world.

H. Byron Earhart
Series Editor

Preface

This book attempts to explain some basic ideas and practices of Chinese religions in direct and simple language, with lots of examples and analogies. Its basic assumption is that religion is best understood as an aspect of everyday life, as something that makes sense to those who practice it, even if outsiders might be puzzled at first. Most religious activities and feelings are special forms of things many people do and feel, even if they are not religious, so all have an opportunity to understand if they wish. Of course, someone who does not practice a particular religion can't feel about it the same way as a person who does, but with careful study we can go a long way toward understanding and appreciation. The place to begin is to try to let the religion speak for itself without bringing in our own ideas and reactions too soon. Once we better understand what is going on, and why, then we are free to accept, reject or just enjoy without getting involved. The best approach to a different religion or culture is the same as the way we try to relate to another person; polite, attentive and sympathetic, but still having our own point of view. Just as we can learn from friends and teachers, so we can learn from other human traditions, even if it is only to decide that we still like our own better.

As can be seen from the Table of Contents, there is material here on Chinese history, religious ideas and practices, and on some additional books to read for those interested.

The *pin-yin* romanization system is used for spelling out the sound of Chinese characters as approved by the Chinese government. Wade-Giles spelling appears in parentheses for more familiar names, as "Daoism (Taoism)".

Since this book is focused on traditional China before the twentieth century I tend to use the past tense, but in fact many of the beliefs and practices described are still alive, at least in some Chinese communities. So, past tense here does not necessarily mean no longer present.

I hope you enjoy the book.

D. L. O.

1

Acknowledgments

My mother has been urging me to write a book like this for a long time, so I dedicate it to her. She deserves it anyway for teaching me five of my first eight grades while our family lived in China during and after World War II. I also want to thank my brother-in-law, Lynn Wilbur, and Randy Nadeau, who read through the manuscript and made several helpful suggestions. Thanks as well to Rachel Rousseau, Carmen de Silva, and Olga Betts of the University of British Columbia, who did the typing.

I am grateful to Byron Earhart, the series editor, who asked me to write the book and helped along the way, as well as to the editors at Harper & Row. Of course, without the support of my family and the University of British Columbia, I would not have the time or energy to write at all.

D. L. O.

"If we dance, it will rain."

*(Shang dynasty oracle bone
inscription, about 1300 B.C.)*

■

Chronology of Chinese History and Religion

Chronology of Chinese Historical Periods and Western Dates

Chronology of Chinese Historical Periods and Western Dates	Major Cultural and Religious Features
Prehistory: Beginning of agricultural village life, c. 6000 B.C.	−grave objects buried with the dead −bone divination (without writing)
Shang dynasty (c. 1500–1040 B.C.)	−rule of a large area by powerful kings −bone and shell divination with written inscriptions −huge tombs with many offerings −rituals by king and priests for ancestors and nature gods
Zhou (Chou) dynasty (1040–256 B.C.)	−China's feudal period; one king with many separate states −ritual feasts for ancestors −"Decree of Heaven" as source of king's authority −first records of shamans and spirit-mediums −search for immortality −rise of philosophy and skepticism about religion for a few
Qin (Ch'in) dynasty (221–207 B.C.)	

Han (or former or
Western Han) dynasty,
(202 B.C.–A.D. 9)

Xin (Hsin) dynasty
(A.D. 9–23)

Later Han (or Eastern Han)
dynasty, (A.D. 25–220)

–beginnings of Chinese empire
  and imperial state religion
–Confucianism established as
  official teaching
–rise of popular religious
  movements
–Buddhism enters China

Three Kingdoms era
(A.D. 220–280)

  Wei (220–266),
  Shu Han (221–263),
  Wu (222–280)

Jin (Chin) (or Western Jin)
dynasty (266–316)

Era of North-South division
(316–589)

  Sixteen Kingdoms
  (301–439)

  Northern and Southern
  dynasties (317–589)

–collapse of empire; China divides
  into separate states again
–beginnings of Daoist religion
–Buddhism becomes established at
  all levels of society

Chronology of Chinese Historical Periods and Western Dates	Major Cultural and Religious Features
Sui dynasty (581–618)	
Tang dynasty (618–907)	—China reunified —Buddhism and Daoism reach a peak of development, with many monasteries and temples —development of Chinese Buddhist philosophy —formation of Pure Land and Chan (Zen) Buddhism —Confucian reaction and the suppression of Buddhist monasteries in the ninth century
Five Dynasties era (907–970)	—another period of political disunity
Song (Sung) (or Northern Song) dynasty (960–1127)	
Northern Conquest dynasties (916–1234)	
Liao dynasty (916–1125)	
Jin (Chin) dynasty (1115–1234)	—China reunified once again, but with threats from other kingdoms to the north —revival of Confucian philosophy —spread of Buddhist devotional societies among the people —Chan becomes the major form of monastic Buddhism

Chronology of Chinese Historical Periods and Western Dates	Major Cultural and Religious Features
Southern Song dynasty (1127–1279)	−North China ruled by the Jurchen (Jin) dynasty −continued development of Confucian thought −popular religion takes shape as a tradition in its own right
Yuan dynasty (1264–1368), Mongol	−all of China conquered by the Mongols −popular religious sects take their characteristic form
Ming dynasty (1368–1644)	−Mongols driven out and replaced by a Chinese emperor −Roman Catholic missionaries in China
Qing (Ch'ing) dynasty (1644–1912), Manchu	−Manchus rule China −continued development of Buddhism, Daoism, and popular religious sects −gradual suppression of Catholicism −invasion of China by European powers in the nineteenth century −Protestant missionaries arrive and Catholics return
Republic of China (1912–1949 on mainland, 1945 to the present in Taiwan), and	

Chronology of Chinese Historical Periods and Western Dates	Major Cultural and Religious Features
People's Republic of China, (1949 to the present)	—collapse of the Qing empire and the rise of a new China —invasion by Japan —civil war between Nationalists and Communists —Communist victory in 1949; Nationalists retreat to Taiwan —popular religion flourishes in Taiwan —suppression of religion during the Cultural Revolution in China, 1966–1976 —restoration of some religious activities after 1978

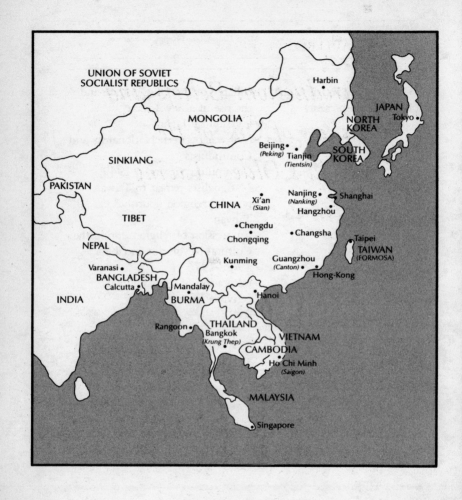

■

CHAPTER I

Introduction: Beliefs and Values of One of the World's Oldest Living Cultures

The feng-shui master, followed by the oldest son of the Liu family, walked up the wooded hillside, pausing now and then to look at the view below. They went over a ridge, and there below them was a small meadow with a creek running across its lower edge. The meadow, facing south, was bathed in sunshine. The master paused and looked back along the ridge; the point where they stood was the end of a long series of hills connected to the mountains in the distance. He went down into the meadow and dug into the soil with a trowel; the soil was dark and crumbled in his hands, and it was covered with grass and wildflowers. He looked down the slope; the view was beautiful and made him feel peaceful and comfortable within. Behind him, the ridge blocked the north winds, which would soon be turning cold. He turned and said, "This is the spot"; this was the place to bury the young man's father. Here his spirit would be at peace.

Back in the village, the son consulted a fortune-teller to decide on a good day for the funeral. The fortune-teller asked him the date and hour of his father's birth in order to calculate which cosmic power was strongest then and to choose a day when that power would be strong again. The best time for the funeral would be *ji-mao* day of the sixty-day cycle, the fourteenth of the next lunar

11

month. Burial then would reinforce the power of Mr. Liu's spirit and make him even more inclined to bless his family. The master laid out the horseshoe-shaped tomb facing south down the hill, set to catch and hold the fertile powers of the meadow. On the fourteenth day, the funeral procession arrived, and the coffin was aligned with the auspicious direction of the year, symbolized by the constellation Mao, the Pleiades. A rectangular wooden tablet about a foot long was laid on its top as a place for the soul to reside. When the ritual was finished and the soul tablet blessed, the Liu family took it home, put it on the altar, and feasted before it to celebrate their new **ancestor**.* They felt satisfied. They had done their job; death had been put in its proper place, and life could go on, guided by memories of the old man and his ancestors many generations before.

This is a story of **feng-shui**, "wind and water," the art of locating graves and houses so that they benefit from cosmic forces in the sky and landscape. Scenes like this have been repeated millions of times in China for the last two thousand years and can still be observed in Taiwan and Hong Kong. Feng-shui puts in practice an ancient Chinese way of looking at the world, a way that assumes that the world is a living system in which everything is connected by shared rhythms and resonances, like instruments in a symphony orchestra. Just as the clear notes of the flute are echoed by the violins and punctuated by drums, so human beings and their world naturally respond to each other, the Chinese have believed, sharing the same notes on different instruments, made of different forms of the same stuff. These rhythms are discussed as the cold, dark forces of **yin** and the hot, bright forces of **yang**; together with the **five powers** of metal, plant life, water, fire, and earth; these forces are modes of **qi**, "vital substance." Their interaction produces all things.

From about 100 B.C. until the mid-twentieth century, most Chinese assumed that this system is simply the way the world is, just as we today assume it is composed of atoms, molecules, electrical forces, and gravity. In China, from an even earlier time, it has been taken for granted that human beings are a natural and necessary part of the world around them; hence, what they do influences nature, and nature in turn is full of significance for them. So, on the longest night of the year in December the emperor would sacrifice a red (yang) bullock on an outdoor altar south of the capital to make

---

*Terms defined in the Glossary are printed in boldface where they first appear in the text.

sure that the yang force of warmth and life would revive. When spring came, he wore green robes to encourage the growth of plant life. Executions had to be reserved for autumn, the time of harvest and cutting down; otherwise the seasons would be disrupted. Peasants, too, offered sacrifices: to gods symbolizing fertility, for example, or power over diseases caused by cosmic forces out of balance. Most Chinese religions and philosophies have been based on this lively view of the world, whatever else they have taught. They assume that the world itself is a sacred place of power and mystery, and that to human beings belongs the important task of cooperating with this power and making it operative within society. This understanding they shared with other traditional cultures, such as that of Japan and those of the native peoples of America, Africa, and Australia. In China, however, philosophers and religious leaders wrote sophisticated books about these ideas long ago, books that have continued to be studied up to the twentieth century. In recent decades scholars all over the world have been studying traditional Chinese religion and philosophy more than ever before. This book is an introduction to what they have learned.

Along with India, China is the oldest literate civilization that has continued to exist right down into the twentieth century. Though there were preliterate tribes in the area of what we now call China many thousands of years ago, the first sophisticated civilization in that part of the world was the Shang kingdom, which appeared about 1500 B.C. Properly speaking, history begins with written records, and this was the beginning of Chinese history. Since the Sumerians and Egyptians developed comparable civilizations about 1500 years before that, China is not the oldest culture, it has just lasted a long time. It is as if the Babylonian kingdom established by Hammurabi in 1750 B.C. were still active today, with its ancient language and social ideas still largely intact. One of the factors that helped Chinese culture survive was religious beliefs that taught that the world makes sense and that human beings have an important responsibility to help hold it together. Many of these beliefs go back to prehistory but have been developed by centuries of thought and writing, writing that millions of people can still read today (much more easily than we can read Latin or Old English).

China was attacked by the British in 1839 and invaded by France, Russia, Germany, and Japan later in the nineteenth century. Since that time, China's economy and society have been changing under foreign impact. A revolution in 1911 overthrew the last emperor and established a republic. The Japanese invaded again in 1931 and 1937, and then came the devastation of World War II. After the war, China was torn apart by a civil war between Communists and Nationalists, a war that the Communists won. They established the People's Republic of China in 1949, and the Nationalists retreated to Taiwan, an island ninety miles off the south China coast. In both China and Taiwan there has been even more rapid change since 1949, both because of communism and because of the impact of modern knowledge and technology. And yet, despite 150 years of change, many of the basic values of Chinese life have remained. Religious beliefs have been strongly criticized on the China mainland for over thirty years, and many **temples** and images have been destroyed; yet even there a strong sense of family loyalty remains, and ancestor worship and traditional funerals have been making a comeback since a period of liberalization began in 1978. In Taiwan, not only are the old religions thriving, but many new religious sects have sprung up, with their own books of scripture and brighly painted temples. There, people who work in factories and offices during the

Home altar. Vertical inscription on the left says: "May the ancestors long aid their descendants." On the right: "May the power of the Buddha forever support the peace and prosperity of this family."

day, drive automobiles, and watch television still worship the old gods and venerate the teachings of **Confucius**, who lived twenty-five hundred years ago, just as modern people in North America and Europe still read the Bible and believe its teachings.

Our deepest hopes and fears are expressed in our religious beliefs and activities. So it is that a study of Chinese religions tells us much about the fundamental attitudes and values of the Chinese people. Through such study we also learn of different points of view, challenging us to think more clearly about our own values. For example, one important Chinese characteristic is remembering and honoring ancestors through simple acts of worship, such as offering sticks of burning incense before wooden tablets with ancestors' names on them, on the family altar. Many Chinese have also kept records of their families for generations, records that are read to young people to remind them of what their ancestors did and stood for. In this way, each generation is taught to be grateful and loyal to the family tradition and to work hard to keep it going. This emphasis may have contributed to the economic success today of countries like Taiwan, Japan, and South Korea, where the old Chinese-style family loyalty is still strong. In such cultures many young people have a sense that they are working for something bigger than themselves; therefore, they study hard and strive to succeed. Of course, sometimes an individual is prevented by the demands of family from doing what he or she wants to do, as in the case of a university graduate who wants to study art but is expected to take over the family's business instead. On the whole, however, the Chinese-style family has worked well for a long time. Perhaps we can learn something from the gratitude and mutual support between family members that keep this system strong. At the least, thinking about it gives us a fresh perspective on the more individualistic tradition of the West.

Another potential contribution to our own thinking is the Chinese sense of the world itself as a holy place, a place that human beings should honor and protect. For example, in a popular religious book called the *Earth Mother Scripture (Di-mu jing)*, the earth is considered a goddess, who says,

> All the **Buddhas** of the three worlds arise from me,
> and **bodhisattvas** do not depart from the body of the Mother.
> All the gods are not separate from me;

if they left me, where would they rest?
The four directions, continents, and seasons were all created by me.
Rivers, lakes, and seas do not exist apart from me.
I produced all states and continents. . . .
I created mountains and forests,
and produced the five grains and six kinds of rice. . . .
When people are alive they eat me,
and when they die they return to my bosom.
Prefectures and counties do not exist apart from me;
temples and monasteries are formed of my body.

After bewailing the fact that people have forgotten their debt to
Mother Earth, the text continues with passages like the following:

If every household will reverence Mother Earth,
there will be an abundant harvest of the five grains,
and peace and joy [will come].
[For them] there will be no great disasters or calamities,
and pious men and women will enjoy health and tranquility.
However if they do not listen to Mother Earth's instructions,
there will be no harvest, and not enough to eat. . . .

This sort of reverence for the earth has obvious parallels with
modern ecology; both ecology and Chinese religion understand the
world to be a product of delicately balanced forces that we interfere
with at our peril, since we are part of it ourselves. The Bible also
teaches that the world is created and loved by God and is to be
properly cared for by human beings, but sometimes Christians and
Jews have forgotten this. A study of Chinese religions can help remind us of important emphases in our own tradition.

The chapters that follow discuss the history of Chinese religions
and some of their distinctive ideas and themes. There is also a look
at how Chinese people actually practice religion today. At the end
there is a list of helpful books to read for those who want to learn
more. The basic concerns of this book are, first, to understand Chinese religions in their own right, and then to see what might be
learned from them.

CHAPTER II

History: The Development of Chinese Religious Traditions Over Time

S ince about 200 B.C. China has been one of the largest and most populous countries in the world, with about 60 million people by A.D. 100. At that time the population of the whole Roman Empire was about the same size, but that empire consisted of a number of smaller countries. Today China is the third largest country in area, after the Soviet Union and Canada, with a population of over one billion, about one fifth of humanity. China extends from the Pacific Ocean to India and Afghanistan, and from Burma in the south to Siberia in the north (see map). Of course, in such a huge area there are many differences in geography and climate, the most important of which are the differences between the regions north and south of the Yangtze River, which divides China in half. As one moves north from the Yangtze, the countryside becomes drier and colder, and there is a large plain around the capital, Beijing (Peking). The most important crops on this northern plain are wheat and millet. In the south, there is more rain, and more rivers and lakes, and the most important crop is rice, which needs large quantities of water. Beijing, in the north, has cold winters with snow, but the climate is quite different in southern China, where it is warm and humid. Still different is western China, which is a desert area with minimal rainfall and vegetation.

A Summary of Chinese History

There have been people in China for at least five hundred thousand years, and by about eight thousand years ago there were many different tribes, some of which had begun to grow grain and vegetables and to raise such domestic animals as chickens, pigs, and dogs. These people lived in small, mud-brick villages surrounded by their fields. Their physical appearance was similar to that of modern Chinese. As time passed, some of these villages grew larger, with walls, houses on earthen platforms, pottery factories, and markets. Since some houses and graves were more elaborate than others, we know that there were a few villagers who had more wealth and power, perhaps even chiefs who occasionally led attacks against other villages. Why would they need walls, except for defense?

Around 1500 B.C. some tribal chiefs on the northern plain had gained so much power that they were able to impose a new form of social organization, a powerful state, led by hereditary kings, called the Shang kingdom after the name of one of its capital cities. This state was run by aristocrats with large landholdings of their own and had an army that controlled the people and attacked surrounding tribes for territory, booty, and prisoners to use as slaves and sacrificial offerings. The Shang elite developed writing to record their petitions to their ancestors and gods and also invented a sophisticated method of casting bronze, which they used to make elaborate bowls, swords and spearheads, and many other objects. These activities were carried out in cities, with buildings and walls much larger than ever before. However, most of the ordinary people continued to be farmers in small villages, using stone tools as their ancestors had done for thousands of years.

One of the powerful neighboring tribes whose name often appears in Shang writings was the Zhou (Chou), who lived to the west of the Shang area. The Zhou alternately fought and traded with the Shang for centuries, gradually learning and gaining strength. Finally, about 1040 B.C., they completely defeated the Shang and took over their kingdom. With the Zhou China entered a feudal period many centuries before similar developments in Europe, a period in which the kings ruled over nobles with semi-independent territories of their own, all of them holding power by inherited right, usually passed on from fathers to eldest sons. The nobles vowed loyalty to the king and every year came to his court with gifts. The king in turn was responsible for settling disputes and for assisting the lords when they were attacked by non-Zhou tribes. Some of the common people were artisans or merchants in the cities, but most were serf farmers who did not own land but worked for the feudal lords for a place to live and the grain they were allowed to keep.

This early Zhou feudal system lasted for about three hundred years, but in the eighth century B.C. some of the lords started to become more independent. A Zhou king was assassinated in 771, after which real power passed into the hands of the lord who was strongest at any given time. Soon civil wars broke out among the many small states, which formed alliances for protection. The Zhou kings continued to rule their own little domain, but not much else. The period of competition and warfare between independent states lasted for several hundred years. Many of the smaller states were swallowed up, so that by 300 B.C. only seven large ones were left. One of these was Qin (Ch'in), in the far west, which was very well organized and had been steadily growing in power. In 256 B.C. Qin took over the royal domain, thus ending the Zhou period, and by 221 it had conquered all the remaining states and set itself up as an empire that included much of what we now call China. Our name *China* comes from the word *Ch'in*.

The first emperor of Qin worked very hard to control China by unifying laws and ways of writing, building the Great Wall, and raising large armies to attack non-Chinese tribes. But many people still remained loyal to the customs of their old states, which were now just provinces run by governors appointed by the emperor. In addition, the Qin public work projects and military campaigns caused a lot of dislocation and suffering, so that just a few years after the Qin empire was founded, rebellions broke out against it. The eventual victor in this new civil war was a former village head named Liu Bang (pron. "Bong"), who set himself up as emperor of a new dynasty, the Han, in 202 B.C.. Except for one fourteen-year break, the Liu family ruled China for the next 408 years. The Han rulers were less harsh than the Qin, but continued many of their innovations, such as abolishing feudal principalities in favor of provinces run by appointed officials. They also took over much of the Qin law code, which was supposed to apply to everybody, including former nobles, and they continued to let people buy and sell their own land. It was during the early Han period that China settled down and became the large, semicontinental state it is today. It is no accident that when Chinese refer to themselves as an ethnic group, they use the name *Han-ren*, "people of the Han."

Han rule was relatively stable for a long time, certainly a big improvement over the civil wars that preceded it. Between A.D. 9 and 23 the Liu line was temporarily displaced by a rebellious prime minister, but the Han dynasty was re-established in A.D. 25. However, in the second century A.D. the government started to lose its grip because of weak emperors who neglected their business and because of quarreling among groups of officials at court. Protests and rebellions broke out, culminating in a huge uprising by a religious sect called the **Yellow Turbans** in 184 (to be discussed later). By this time the imperial army was too disorganized to defeat the Yellow Turbans, so the emperor encouraged provincial governors to raise militia armies to do the job. This policy worked, and the uprising was put down in a few months; but when the dust settled there were several victorious provincial armies that the governors wanted to hang on to. The result was civil war between these provincial warlords, which led to the fall of the Han dynasty in A.D. 220. From then until 581 China was politically divided, first between three kingdoms in the north, southeast, and southwest that immediately succeeded the Han. Now, however, each state claimed the right to re-establish the empire, the unity of which always remained an ideal.

China had long been threatened by nomadic tribes from inner Asia, which was too dry and cold for agriculture. In A.D. 311 and 317 two northern Chinese capitals were captured by one of these peoples, the Huns, whose relatives were attacking the Roman Empire at the other end of Asia at the same time. As a result of this conquest non-Chinese clans ruled north China for about 250 years, and many of the Chinese elite fled south across the Yangtze River, where Chinese states held off the invaders. Of course, there were not many nomads in comparison with Chinese, and the nomads were illiterate and not organized to rule a large farming economy, so the inner Asian rulers in the north had no choice but to learn Chinese and administer with the help of Chinese officials. Before long they became culturally Chinese themselves, and Chinese religions continued to develop in the north as well as the south during this "period of disunion."

In the late sixth century a northern ruler named Yang Jian conquered the south and reunified China in the Sui dynasty, beginning in 581. However, Sui rule was too abrupt and harsh, as the Qin had been centuries before, so it lasted only until 618. By then there had been another long period of rebellion and civil war; the victors, a family named Li, set up a new dynasty, the Tang, in 618. Just as the Han rulers had done, they strengthened the unity enforced by their predecessors and established the foundation for a long period of peace and prosperity. From then on, China alternated between periods of political unity and disunity, and rule by Chinese or central Asian peoples. After the Tang there was half a century of disunity between north and south (see chronological chart), and then China was reunited again by the Song (Sung) dynasty, from 960 to 1127. The north was then taken over again by peoples from what are now Manchuria and Mongolia. In the thirteenth and fourteenth centuries the country was united for ninety years by the Mongols under Chinggis Khagan (Genghis Khan), who by that time had an empire stretching all the way to Europe. However, by 1368 several Chinese rebel armies had driven out the Mongols, and the victorious general set up a new dynasty, the Ming, which established a period of unity that lasted until the revolution of 1911. After 1644, the unified China was again ruled by a non-Han people, the Manchus, who called their dynasty the Qing (Ch'ing). So it was that imperial Chinese history ended with rulers of non-Chinese origin on the throne, though the Manchus had become quite Chinese in their language and customs.

Chinese Society

Thus, for the first 1700 years of their history the Chinese ruled themselves in the Shang, Zhou, and Han. They had contacts with other people and traded with them, but foreigners had very little impact on Chinese culture, which pretty much developed by itself. Beginning in about A.D. 300, central Asian peoples began what became a long history of occasionally ruling part or all of China. These tribes—originally illiterate and technologically and socially less developed than the Chinese, though superior at horse-mounted warfare—despite their military power, had little influence on Chinese culture and ideas. Instead, after the tribal peoples took over, they were assimilated into China and sometimes even forgot their own language and dress. The most important exceptions to this pattern of assimilation were the coming of Buddhism from India in the first century A.D. and the invasions by Europeans in the nineteenth century. In both cases, Chinese culture was slowly influenced by foreign ideas.

So, for the most part, Chinese culture and religion developed on their own terms, the product of centuries of village agricultural life. To be sure, social divisions appeared between men and women, rich and poor, aristocrats and commoners, but these divisions evolved locally out of the same peasant base. For the first 1800 years of its history China was never successfully invaded by foreigners whose nobility took over the country as happened in such places as India, Britain, and Mexico. Even later invaders, such as the Manchus, relied on Chinese officials. This means that at a cultural level the split between rulers and people, aristocrats and peasants, was not as sharp as it was in some other countries. In China even the elite who lived in cities usually had family farms in the countryside. Everyone assumed the same world view: everyone venerated ancestors, practiced feng-shui, carried out funerals, enjoyed the same annual festivals. Other factors influenced this relatively high degree of cultural integration. One was printing, which was used to publish books in China as early as the ninth century A.D., six hundred years before the first printed book in Europe. In China printing spread rapidly, particularly after the twelfth century. This meant that knowledge was not confined to a tiny elite but was available to anyone who could read, and until the nineteenth century a higher percentage of Chinese could read than could Europeans.

Another integrating factor was written civil service examinations, which were established in the sixth century A.D. There were several levels of these examinations, from the county to the capital city. Those who passed were given degrees, and also given government offices when they were available, and in old China government service was the chief way to power and prestige. Except for a few categories, such as beggars and criminals, all Chinese men were eligible to take these examinations and progress as far as they could. Small schools were set up in most towns to help them prepare. To be sure, the sons of rich families often did better because they could afford private tutors, but the examination system was still a big change from the days when aristocrats passed government offices around among themselves and their sons. This change meant that there was more opportunity for men to move up or down the social system, depending on their wits, energy, and luck. The examinations were based on a set of Confucian books that everyone had to study, usually in the form of preparation manuals like those Americans use for college entrance examinations. This meant that ideas and values supported by the state were memorized by people throughout society, further contributing to cultural integration.

At another level this integration was encouraged by the network of outdoor markets in villages and towns to which people came from a wide area to shop, get haircuts, worship at temples, go to popular operettas, listen to storytellers, and exchange news. In larger markets there would be people from other parts of China, or even foreign merchants. Through these market networks people learned that they were part of a larger society with many common customs and values. All of this makes it possible for us to discuss points of unity among Chinese religions.

Of course, there were many differences and tensions as well. Then, as now, each local area in China had its own dialect, which people from elsewhere often could not understand, though everyone who could read and write used the same written language. Each area also had its own particular customs and foods and special gods and heroes. Even after the civil service examination system took effect, those who passed looked down on those who did not, and there were sharp differences between rich and poor. Most of the people had to struggle every day just to survive, and they were often oppressed by high taxes and rents, greedy landlords, and corrupt officials. Educated religious leaders tended to despise the beliefs and rituals of the common people, even though members of their own families usually practiced them. Such leaders sometimes criticized each other's religions as well. Any kind of organized religious sect was outlawed by the state, particularly after the thirteenth century, and there were laws as well against spirit-mediums and some forms of divination. In sum, there were enough differences to provide variety, but enough common ground so that China may be discussed in general terms as one culture.

As has been true for many traditional societies, in China the family was the basic unit of ownership, economic activity, and prestige. Individual differences were recognized, but for the most part individual interests were subordinated to those of the family. Fathers had the highest authority, and families were known by their surnames. Sons were to continue the family line, and often followed their fathers' occupations. Women had some rights, but they were basically in an inferior position, and didn't become full-fledged members of society until they married and had sons. Since the family was so central (and still is), it is not surprising that the single most important religious activity was ancestor worship, the veneration of predecessors in the father's line of descent, beginning with his parents. The spirits of ancestors were believed to live on, and had power to bless or curse their descendants, depending on how they were treated. Living and dead were connected together in one stream; the living were to uphold the family traditions, bring honor to their ancestors, and prepare for becoming good ancestors themselves, remembered for their work and example. Descendants were expected to offer food and incense regularly before wooden tablets inscribed with the names of their parents, grandparents, and earlier predecessors. These offerings revived the power of the spirits, and encouraged them to aid their families. Such ancestor worship is reflected in the earliest records of Chinese religions, and is a fundamental connecting point in the Chinese view of the world. Once the realms of the living and dead were understood to be so intimately related, other sorts of relationships were easy to accept as well.

A Brief History of Chinese Religious Beliefs and Activities

Prehistory and the Early Period

Archaeologists have found some evidence of prehistoric religious activities, before the Shang dynasty. Most tombs included offerings such as tools, pottery vessels, and jade ornaments, which indicate belief that the dead could use such objects in some form of afterlife. Graves were often located in clusters and lined up in rows near villages, suggesting a special relationship between the living and the dead. Some people buried deer in fields, presumably as offerings to the power of fertility in the soil. **Divination** was also practiced by heating dried shoulder bones of sheep or deer and reading answers to yes-or-no questions through the patterns of the cracks. In the light of later practices we know more about, it looks as if prehistoric Chinese already venerated their ancestors, tried to discover their will through divination, and made offerings to powers of nature.

For the Shang period we have evidence for the religion of the king and aristocracy but not for the common people, except for grave objects, as before. The king was the chief priest and diviner of the realm, and the results of his bone-cracking divination were often inscribed on the bone after the process was completed (the bottom shells of turtles were also used). For example, on the right and left sides of a shell there might be such inscriptions as, "The king's toothache is caused by Ancestor Jie," and "Perhaps the king's toothache is not caused by Ancestor Jie," with an indication of which alternative was indicated by the cracks and which came true. It was usually ancestors who were consulted, but sometimes nature gods of rivers or mountains, and in a few cases, **Shang-di**, "The Ruler Above," the chief god of the Shang state (which is written with a different character).

Shang diviners also inquired about the weather, harvests, warfare, and many other topics. The king and his priests offered regular sacrifices to ancestors and to gods believed to live in the air, water, and the earth. Such offerings included jade thrown into rivers, wine poured out on the earth, and flesh and grain burned on open-air altars. It was assumed that if the offering was properly made, the god or ancestor had to respond.

Shang kings were buried in huge pit tombs several yards wide, with all sorts of grave offerings, including not only implements of bronze and jade but also dogs, horses, and decapitated human beings. It was believed that at death kings could enjoy the same luxuries they had in life, perhaps in heaven with their ancestors and Shang-di. Of course, we know of similar royal tombs all over the world, from ancient Egypt, Africa, Persia, and many other places.

For the religion of the early Zhou period we have more detailed records, such as the *Shi-jing, "The Book of Poetry,"* which was composed by 600 B.C. From these materials we know that Zhou nobles honored their ancestors with great feasts in which the ancestor was represented by a nephew or grandson who had to dress and act in a very formal manner. First, petitions were read, then everyone ate and drank to the full; they believed such ritual meals should be joyous occasions. The Zhou continued to offer sacrifices and to divine much as the Shang had done, but they had a better developed understanding of their high-god, whom they called **Tian (T'ien)**, "Heaven." The Zhou founders proclaimed that Tian had chosen them to replace the Shang because the last Shang kings were corrupt and no longer took proper care of the people, who were really the "people of Heaven." This new theory was that of the "Decree of Heaven" (Tian-ming): Every ruler was given authority by Heaven, but only so long as he was compassionate and just. If he failed, the divine right to rule could be transferred to someone else. The "Decree of Heaven" idea has been important in Chinese history ever since because it imposes an ethical and religious check on the king's behavior and provides a basis for criticism of him by officials and the people. Over the centuries many rebellions have been led by men who claimed the "Decree of Heaven" for themselves.

The Zhou kings had a religious title, "Son of Heaven" (Tian-zi, T'ien-tzu), which indicates how important their task was; they were Heaven's representatives on earth. As such, they were responsible both for the people and for the powers of nature as they affected human life. A large part of the king's time was spent performing rituals to make sure that the ancestors and gods were satisfied, that rains would come and crops would grow. The king had a vital role in the balance of cosmic forces; failure to perform the proper ritual at the right time could bring disaster, as could bad laws or cruelty by royal officials. So it was that the kings appointed officers to report on any unusual happenings in the realm, like earthquakes, comets, epidemics, or rebellions; any such disturbance could mean that things were out of balance because the king was doing something wrong. If he was, then he had to repent before Heaven and do something to make up for it, such as freeing prisoners or reducing taxes.

Some Zhou court officials had special responsibility for assisting with rituals and divination, but there was no separate organization or "church" for priests. However, other religious specialists were sometimes brought to court, shamans or **spirit-mediums**, persons who believed they could be possessed by gods or ancestral spirits. It was thought that spirits temporarily came down into their bodies, spoke through them, and gave them special knowledge of the future or of how to heal illness. Most illness or misfortune was believed to be caused by demons (**gui/kuei**) or ancestral spirits angry because their graves had been neglected or because they were not receiving enough sacrificial offerings to sustain their energy. Because shamans could talk to such spirits, they could identify the cause of a problem and suggest what to do about it, such as rebuilding a grave. These shamans were not aristocrats, but commoners with special skills, much in demand by both the court and ordinary folk. By the fifth century A.D., shamans were gradually forced out of court rituals by officials, who thought they were too emotional and hard to control, but they continued to be active among the general population and still are in Taiwan and the Chinese countryside. They are folk psychiatrists and healers who try to cure illnesses that do not respond to other forms of medical care.

In the early Zhou period, all the feudal domains had their own rituals and priests, centered on the ancestors of the ruler and on mountains and rivers, imposing natural forces that were believed to control rainfall. During the long period of civil war that began in the eighth century B.C., many of these domains or states were destroyed, and with them their ancestral temples and shrines to deities of mountains and rivers. The ancestors and deities were supposed to protect the state, but clearly many of them failed. The same could be said of Heaven, which was expected to preserve prosperity and peace for those who ruled properly. Thus, for a few intellectuals, destructive warfare led to questions about the gods and spirits. Maybe they weren't so powerful after all. Perhaps there were natural explanations for storms and earthquakes. Perhaps demons were just imagined by people when they were really afraid. Questions such as these helped prepare for a new way of thinking that concentrated more on human beings and less on spirit world. The first well-known representative of this new approach was Confucius (551–479 B.C.).

The Rise of Philosophy

Confucius was the son of an obscure family in the small state of Lu, a state in which the old Zhou cultural traditions were strong but that had been repeatedly upset by invasions and by struggles between local clans. Confucius was concerned about restoring peace and order and studied old books, rituals, and legends to look for guidelines for the present. He came to realize that what was needed were moral principles that applied to everyone, principles, such as justice, honesty, and love, that could be followed in all situations. He believed that these principles were the will of Heaven for human beings, in particular, for the ruler and his officials, who were supposed to rule for the benefit of the people.

The highest goal for such leaders was to develop an inner sense of ethical commitment, *ren (jen)*, deep empathy and compassion for others. This inward power of concern was to be expressed in everyday life as reverence for parents, loyalty to friends, and care for the common people, all carried out in a balanced harmonious way *(li)*. Ethically educated persons were to be honest, frugal and hard-working, always trying to improve society and government.

Confucius never did obtain a high office in Lu from which he could put his teachings into practice, but he soon gathered a small group of disciples whom he taught to be "superior persons" *(jun-zi)*, educated men with high principles who would be good government officials. For him, what counted was intelligence and dedication, not inherited aristocratic status. Confucius claimed he was just restoring old ideas, but actually he was a reformer who introduced new ethical concepts and a new type of education and reinforced the policy of appointing good men to office whether they were aristocrats or not.

There were two sides to Confucius' religious views. On the one hand, he paid no attention to such practices as shamanism and divination, which he thought were beneath the dignity of a "superior person." On the other hand, Confucius had a deep personal sense of loyalty to Heaven, which he felt had given him a mission to reform the world. After he died, Confucius' disciples remembered his teachings and eventually put them together into a book, the *Discourses and Sayings (Lun-yu)*. In this book we read that on a few occasions when Confucius' life was in danger he fell back on his faith in Heaven to keep his confidence and sense of destiny.

For example, once a powerful official named Huan Tui tried to have Confucius assassinated, probably because the philosopher had criticized his policies. When Confucius was warned, he said, "Heaven begat the power that is in me. What have I to fear from such a one as Huan Tui?"

Because he was never appointed to an important position, Confucius felt that no one appreciated his ability, but here also his sense of mission from Tian gave him confidence. As he once said, "The truth is no one knows me. . . . I do not accuse heaven nor lay the blame on men. But the studies of men here below are felt on high, and perhaps after all I am known; not here, but in heaven."[1]

After Confucius, many other thinkers taught methods of saving the world from warfare and disorder. Most of them also had disciples whom they trained to obtain government office and put their ideas into practice. Since most of the rulers of the mid-Zhou period were corrupt and power hungry, this was no easy task, but the philosophers kept trying. Most of them retained a sense that the world was a holy place that should be ordered and peaceful, but their teachings became more and more practical in order to catch the attention of rulers. In the process, most language about Heaven, the gods, and rituals dropped out of sight; these philosophers were concerned almost entirely with human society and government. One group of thinkers, the Authoritarians, simply talked about how the ruler could become more powerful by centralizing and organizing his administration.

The Confucians, however, kept their sense of Heaven's will, as did a philosopher named **Mo-zi (Mo-tzu**, fifth century B.C.), who taught that Heaven had created the world, loved its people, and wanted them to be prosperous and at peace. In practice, Heaven's love meant material and social benefits for the people, such as food, land, and mutual caring for each other. Several of Mo-zi's disciples obtained government positions during his lifetime, worked hard to follow his teachings, and reported back to him what they had accomplished. Mo-zi's belief in Heaven's love is well expressed in the following passage:

> Moreover, I know for the following reason that Heaven loves the people generously: It sets forth one after another the sun and moon, the stars and constellations, to lighten and lead them; it orders the four seasons, spring, fall, winter, and summer, to regulate their lives; it sends down snow and frost, rain and dew, to nourish the five grains, hemp, and silk, so that the people may enjoy the benefit of them. It lays out the mountains and rivers, the ravines and valley streams, and makes known all affairs so as to ascertain the good or evil of the people. It establishes kings and lords to reward the worthy and punish the

wicked, to gather together metal and wood, birds and beasts, and to seek the cultivation of the five grains, hemp, and silk, so that the people may have enough food and clothing. From ancient times to the present this has always been so.[2]

In the fourth and third centuries B.C., some thinkers appeared who tried a different approach, that of noninterference (*wu-wei*), letting things be in their natural state. This approach was first discussed in two books, called the ***Lao-zi (Lao-tzu)*** and ***Zhuang-zi (Chuang-tzu)***, which were written by disillusioned intellectuals who thought that all the various theories of improving the world only made things worse, because they all depended on telling other people what to do. These books teach that everything in the world is produced by the cosmic Way **(Dao/Tao)**, which also provides harmony and balance. Because of this Way, things are just fine in their natural state and should be left alone, from plants and animals to people. The eternal Way of the universe is far wiser than any person could possibly be, so it is always a mistake for us to try to change things around. All we are doing is asserting our own egos and trying to substitute our own limited knowledge for the wisdom of the universe. So it was that the writers of the *Lao-zi* and *Zhuang-zi* taught that the best rulers were those who left the people alone, because they could prosper by themselves. They know how to act even without being taught such high-sounding moral principles as righteousness and respect for elders. Indeed, advocating such principles shows that one probably does not have them!

The *Lao-zi* and *Zhuang-zi* have very little to say about gods or rituals, but they do have a strong sense of the mystery and power of the universal Dao that is present everywhere for those who know how to look. These books are thus important sources for Chinese cosmic mysticism, a sense of personal identification with the basic forces of the universe. We can get an idea of this sense of mystery from passages like the following:

There was something undifferentiated and yet complete,
　　Which existed before heaven and earth.
Soundless and formless, it depends on nothing and does not change.
It operates everywhere and is free from danger.
It may be considered the mother of the universe.

I do not know its name; I call it Tao [Dao].
If forced to give it a name, I shall call it Great.
Now being great means functioning everywhere.
Functioning everywhere means far-reaching.
Being far-reaching means returning to the original point.

The Great Tao flows everywhere.
   It may go left or right.
All things depend on it for life,
   and it does not turn away from them.
It accomplishes its task,
   but does not claim credit for it.
It clothes and feeds all things
   but does not claim to be master over them.
Always without desires, it may be called The Small.
All things come to it and it does not master them;
   it may be called The Great.
Therefore (the sage) never strives himself for the great, and thereby
the great is achieved.[3]

The Dao in this passage sounds a bit like Jewish or Christian concepts of God, but unlike God, Dao has no consciousness or will. It is a way of talking about the world itself as something sacred. The term *sage*, in the second passage refers to the wise ruler who imitates the Dao or way of nature in his administration. He works to help everyone else to find peace and prosperity but does not claim credit for himself. Because he doesn't harass the people with military service and high taxes they accomplish much on their own, and so "the great is achieved."

By the fourth century B.C. there were also philosophers who taught that the universe had developed through the interaction of natural forces such as yin, yang and the five powers or phases. They were the first formulators of the characteristic Chinese world view described in Chapter I. One thinker, **Xun-zi (Hsün-tzu**, d. 215 B.C.), taught that Tian, or Heaven, was not divine at all but was simply a general name for what we would call the laws of nature. It was orderly, but had no will or purpose and had nothing to do with human morality. For Xun-zi, gods and spirits were not real, but just products of human imagination. Rituals and music might be beautiful and inspiring, but were not a matter of pleasing the gods. Xun-zi's skepticism about religion went much further than that of Confucius and helped establish a skeptical tradition in Chinese philosophy that has persisted until today. His views are well illustrated by the following passage.

> You pray for rain and it rains. Why? For no particular reason, I say. It is just as though you had not prayed for rain and it rained anyway. The sun and moon undergo an eclipse and you try to save them;* a drought occurs and you pray for rain; you consult the arts of divination before making a decision on some important matter. But it is not as though you could hope to accomplish anything by such ceremonies. They are done merely for ornament. Hence the gentleman regards them as ornaments, but the common people regard them as supernatural. He who considers them ornaments is fortunate; he who considers them supernatural is unfortunate.[4]

In other words, Xun-zi taught that the educated person should understand religious rituals to be a kind of decoration, not literally true. This was always a minority view in China, but had much influence on how intellectuals looked at religion, especially that of the common people. It was considered vulgar and uneducated to be too enthusiastic about religious beliefs and practices.

The Search for Immortality

While a few philosophers were ignoring religion or redefining it in a more abstract way as identification with "Heaven" or the "Dao," the great majority of the Chinese people continued to practice rituals and divination as they always had. By the fourth century B.C. a set of beliefs appeared that had been developing for a long time, beliefs that there were ways for human beings to escape death, either by living for a very long time or by being reborn in a new form after what only appeared to be death. Methods for attaining such immortality were developed by men called *fang-shi* "technique special-

---

*In ancient China it was believed that eclipses were caused by a great doglike monster in the sky who was eating the sun and moon. Hence, during an eclipse people made a lot of noise to scare the monster away. Xun-zi rejects this practice.

ists," who tried to gain influence and positions in state governments just as the philosophers did. They claimed they had learned techniques for overcoming death from beings who had attained immortality long ago and now lived in paradises on distant mountaintops or islands. These methods were all based on refining and strengthening the qi, or "vital substance," of which we are made. One method involved deep breathing to circulate the breath (qi) in the body; others were exercises based on the movements of long-lived animals like cranes and tortoises. Some fang-shi advocated special vegetarian diets; others advocated drinking compounds of gold and other minerals to make the body as firm and changeless as they were. Chinese religions of this period did not have a very well developed idea of an afterlife; at best, souls of the dead continued to exist for a time in the ancestral tablet, in the grave, or in a dark underground area called the Yellow Springs, which was not very pleasant. Going to Heaven's court was reserved for the royal family; people who wanted to survive death in a more satisfactory way had to work at it and spend a lot of time and money learning immortality techniques. Nonetheless, this hope became quite widespread; there are even stories of whole families ascending to paradise together after they were daubed with an immortality potion by a fang-shi.

During the Qin and Han dynasties several emperors tried to attain immortality themselves and even sent expeditions to look for island paradises. They summoned shamans and fang-shi to court from all over China. In this first period of the Chinese empire, official rituals of all sorts were made more elaborate, and emperors periodically toured the realm, climbing sacred mountains and performing sacrifices to important local deities. They did this both because they believed in divine powers and because they wanted to impress on everybody that all the gods in China were on their side, and therefore the government should be obeyed. Of course, some modern nations still try to claim religious support for their policies in similar ways.

The Beginnings of Daoism (Taoism): Popular Movements in the Late Han (Second Century A.D.)

In 3 B.C. there appeared in China a popular religious movement based on faith in a mother goddess, **Xi Wang-mu**, the "Queen Mother of the West." Many people believed that if they worshiped her and wore charms with her name on them they would not die. This is what some old Chinese history books have to say about the movement:

> [Chien-p'ing], fourth year, spring. There was a severe drought [in the first lunar month: February to March]. In the area east of the passes, the people were exchanging tokens in preparation for the advent of the Queen Mother of the West. They passed through the commanderies and kingdoms, moving west to within the passes and reaching the capital city. In addition persons were assembling to worship the Queen Mother of the West, sometimes carrying fire to the roof-tops by night, beating drums, shouting and frightening one another.
>
> In the first month of the fourth year of Chien-p'ing, the population were running around in a state of alarm, each person carrying a manikin of straw or hemp. People exchanged these emblems with one another, saying that they were carrying out the advent procession. Large numbers of persons, amounting to thousands, met in this way on the roadsides, some with dishevelled hair or going barefoot. Some of them broke down the barriers of gates by night; some clambered over walls to make their way into [houses]; some harnessed teams of horses to carriages and rode at full gallop, setting up relay stations so as to convey the tokens. They passed through twenty-six commanderies and kingdoms, until they reached the capital city.
>
> That summer the people came together in meetings in the capital city and in the commanderies and kingdoms. In the village settlements, the lanes and paths across the fields, they held services and set up gaming boards for a lucky throw, and they sang and danced in worship of the Queen Mother of the West. They also passed round a written message, saying "The Mother tells the people that those who wear this talisman will not die; and let those who do not believe Her words look below the pivots on their gates, and there will be white hairs there to show that this is true."[5]

This movement died out a few months later. We know little of its origins, though the Queen Mother of the West is mentioned in earlier Chinese stories. What is most significant for our understanding of the history of Chinese religions is that here a single, powerful deity promises an easy and simple means of salvation to ordinary people. This is the first such popular religious movement we know of in China. It helped prepare the way for the rise of **Daoism**, China's earliest organized religion, with its own special priests, rituals, and scriptures.

As the Han dynasty started to fall apart in the second century, several popular religious leaders appeared who claimed to have received revelations from gods and immortals, all intended to restore peace and prosperity in China. At first they appealed to the court, but the emperors were not interested, so before long some of these leaders began to proclaim that they had a divine commission to replace the Han with new kingdoms of their own in which everyone would be secure and happy. Since the government considered this treason, several of these men were executed, but others kept on trying. In the 180s a man named Zhang Jue organized a huge popular movement called the Way of Great Peace and Prosperity (Tai-ping dao) and announced that at the beginning of the next sixty-year cycle of time (A.D. 184 by our calendar) the cosmic force of earth would become dominant and replace that of the Han. In that year several thousand of Zhang's followers rebelled in provinces all over north China in an attempt to set up their own utopian kingdom. They came to be called Yellow Turbans, because of the colored cloths they wore to symbolize the power of earth, which has a yellow hue in north China. Their leaders were both priests and military officers at the same time. They taught that illness could be cured by confessing the sins that caused it, and they performed rituals to enlist the gods in bringing immortality to the souls of their ancestors. Their chief deity was the Lord Lao, the legendary author Lao-zi worshiped as a god and believed to be the creator of the world. The Yellow Turbans also had a sacred book, the *Scripture of Great Peace and Prosperity (Tai-ping jing)*, some of which still survives.

The *Tai-ping jing* proclaims itself to be a "celestial book" revealed by a "divine man" to save humankind. This is to be done by restoring good government, which will encourage peace and cooperation in society. To make sure he is on the right track, the ruler is to collect suggestions and complaints from the people in sealed boxes placed all over his kingdom. By setting a good example, he is to transform the people so that they will support each other and help those in need. Those who live in this noncompetitive and noninterfering way are promised good health and long life.

The moral teachings of the *Tai-ping jing* are summarized in the following list of six serious sins and their results:

1. To accumulate Dao, to keep it for oneself, and to refuse to teach it to others for their salvation. Those who commit this fault interrupt the Celestial Dao of life and bring the wrath of Heaven upon them.

2. To accumulate De [inner vitality] and to refuse to teach it to others so that they may nourish their vital principle. This is to interrupt the nourishing De of Earth and to arouse her wrath.

3. To accumulate riches and refuse to help the poor, letting them die of starvation and cold. These goods belong to the Central Harmony, that is to say, to mankind, and they are the means through which Heaven and Earth lavish their blessings. . . . They must circulate so that everyone has what he needs. Those who interrupt this circulation and who hoard what does not belong to them are enemies of the Harmonious Breath of Heaven and Earth.

4. To know that Heaven has a Dao and nevertheless to despise that Dao, to refuse to study it in order to prepare for one's own salvation and obtain long life. This comes to treating with contempt the body which was bequeathed by the ancestors, that is, to be a man without Dao and to be fated to die.

5. To know that it is good to practice De but to make no effort toward the good, to do evil in contempt of oneself. This is to revolt against Earth, which loves De.

6. The person whom Heaven has provided with muscles and physical strength so that he may nourish and clothe himself and who lives in idleness and becomes the parasite of the rich commits a deadly sin, because Heaven and Earth produce the riches necessary for man, who has to draw from them according to his strength and within the limits of his needs. If he does not make any effort and if he cannot obtain from others what he lacks, he will go so far as to seize the goods of others. Then he will be an enemy of the Central Harmony.[6]

The ideal government promoted by the *Tai-ping jing* was never put into practice, but the teachings of this book influenced many generations of Daoists in the centuries that followed. Some of its ideas still make good sense today.

The Yellow Turban uprising was defeated in 184, but there was a similar group in west China at the same time that lasted much longer, The Way of the Celestial Masters *(Tian-shi dao)*. This religious sect set up its own state ruled by a "Celestial Master," Zhang Lu (Chang-lu), who was assisted by priest officials (the Yellow Turbans were similarly organized). The Way of the Celestial Masters also worshiped Lao-zi as a god and recited the book attributed to him as a scripture text. Since members were required to contribute five bushels of rice each year, the nickname for this group was The Way of Five Bushels of Rice. The Celestial Master state lasted until A.D. 215, when it was incorporated into the state of Wei in the north, one of the three kingdoms that succeeded the Han dynasty.

These popular movements in the late Han marked an important new development in the history of Chinese religions, the beginning of religious sects, with their own gods, beliefs, scriptures, rituals, leaders, and organizations, separate from the state and family. Their priests were commoners, yet they claimed to have direct revelations from celestial deities and powers that earlier were supposed to be available only to the emperor and court officials. Thus, these groups marked the beginning in China of a type of religious organization that is still very active all over the world today. They were parallel in time and structure to early Christianity and other sects in the Roman Empire.

The Yellow Turbans and the Way of Five Bushels of Rice were also the forerunners of Daoism, which was the most important religious tradition founded in China (next to the ritual system supported by the government).

The decline of the Han dynasty in the second century A.D. meant that in many areas law and order were not enforced, and state supported rituals not performed. Some officials, fang-shi, and literate farmers responded to this decline by creating their own systems of administration and religion. The Celestial Master state in west China was divided up into twenty-four administrative districts, each led by a "libationer," a priest who was also in charge of all local affairs. These priests performed rituals modeled on those of the old imperial religion. After their state was taken over by Wei, some of these libationers served the Wei court and promised it divine support. At the same time they were the chiefs of religious congregations whose members were promised health and long life. Such benefits could be

A Daoist priest conducts a ritual.

obtained partly through proper diet and exercises, and partly with the help of gods who cooperated with the libationers. So it was that the Celestial Master movement became an established religion in north China.

When the north was invaded by nomadic tribes in the early fourth century A.D., many Chinese aristocrats fled south and took the Celestial Master religion with them. There, around what is now Nanjing (Nanking), they encountered southern religious leaders who had long practiced alchemy and worshiped gods of their own. The southerners were influenced by the Celestial Master religion, but before long a few of them began to have visions of gods who were higher and more mysterious than those of the Celestial Masters. These deities revealed scriptures that were written down in a beautiful flowing script; scriptures that spoke of immortals and star gods who would share secrets of health and perpetual life with those devoted to them. Some of these devotees were appointed by the gods as their special intermediaries or priests and told to warn people that although before long the world would end, a special few could be saved. At about the same time, other intellectuals were writing books about alchemy, mixing herbs or chemicals that could bring long life for someone who was a good person and prepared them properly. Daoism developed out of the combination of these new revelations with alchemy and the older tradition of the Celestial Masters. By the fifth century it had priests who initiated novices to succeed themselves, elaborate rituals, scriptures in classical Chinese, and scores of gods with different levels of power. The scriptures were supposed to be studied only by the priests (as was true of the Latin Bible in medieval Christianity); they contained the names of gods and secret chants for bringing the power of the gods down from the stars and into the body of the priest. Different organs of the body were believed to be residences for these gods. Priests were supposed to prepare for rituals by meditating on the gods and abstaining from sex, wine, and strong-tasting foods. After several months of such preparation, their bodies would be charged with star power, which they could transmit to earth through ritual chants and movements. Thus they could drive away demons, heal illness, and renew the forces of life and fertility in the community that sponsored the ritual. The Daoist priesthood thus provided a means of religious expression and status for educated people and also made cosmic life-power available for ordinary villagers. However, real knowledge of Daoist beliefs and techniques was limited to priests and their initiated disciples. They did not preach sermons to explain things to the people. So Daoism was still elitist, and there were still millions of people in China, educated or not, who were not sure what happened after death, and not sure that in the long run a moral life made sense and was worth the effort. What these people did not have was a religion that provided an organized path of life for everybody, with clear teachings about the fate of the dead, whether good or bad. The Chinese found this sort of egalitarian universal religion in Buddhism.

The Coming of Buddhism

Buddhism was begun in northeastern India in about 500 B.C. by a man named Gautama Siddhartha from the Sakya tribe in the mountains near what is now Nepal. Later on, he came to be called Sakyamuni (Chin. Shi-jia-mou-ni), "the Sage of the Sakyas," and Buddha (Chin. Fo), "the Enlightened One." Gautama studied with a number of spiritual guides, or gurus, to look for a religion that had sensible and satisfactory teachings about suffering, life, and death, but he found them all too one-sided in one way or another. Finally, after years of searching and meditating, he found the answers he wanted in his own mind; he was "enlightened" and immediately started to tell others what he had discovered. What Gautama believed he had found is the way life really is, always changing and full of suffering, yet offering hope to those who accept things as they are and do their best to live a moral life. Most other religions teach that there is something solid and eternal behind the changes of life, something they call God, or Dao, or Brahman (the cosmic soul of Hinduism). But for the Buddha such solidity is an illusion: it is just something we want to believe to feel secure and assure ourselves that we can last forever too. He thought it was better to accept the fact that life is basically impermanent and stop trying to deny the inevitable, ever-changing character of life and death. In his experience such acceptance eventually brought a new peace of mind and a new sense of compassion for other living things, all of whom are caught in the same situation.

The Buddha believed that the reason most people are anxious and fearful is that underneath they are egocentric; that is, they tend to have a narrow and selfish point of view that sees everything as threatening or promising, victory or defeat, just for themselves. So they are always trying to build up their egos, to make them permanent and free from injury or even death. Of course, since the world is always changing, this is an impossible task; our false sense of ego is always threatened and thus makes us a lot more nervous than we need to be. The answer is to meditate on life and affirm its impermanence and change as just the way things have always been. We thus can come to realize that we too are part of the movement of everything else, and so there is really no isolated and fearful ego to fight for. Life just is, and we might as well relax and enjoy it.

Of course, there was more to it than that, because the Buddha also believed that life moves according to regular patterns of cause and effect that the human mind can understand. There is a cause or reason for everything that happens, and every result or effect of one cause in turn becomes the cause of something else. Eventually, everything is related. This was a very advanced idea for 500 B.C.; we would even call it scientific, but the Buddha was more interested in psychology than physics; for him, the point is that our feelings and actions also operate according to laws of cause and effect, which he called **karma**, an Indian word meaning "act" or "deed." For example, if I shout angrily at someone, he or she is likely to shout back; my anger causes his reaction. Or, suppose I want a fancy new machine, like a computer, and feel that it will improve my ability to get a job or good marks and be the envy of my friends. Once the desire for the computer is set in my mind, then I will be happy if I get one and frustrated if I cannot. But in either case the sensation will not last long; I will soon discover that someone else got a better deal or that my computer is out of date, or I will give up the whole idea as too expensive and start wanting something else. Whatever the sensation, it springs from changing desires, and those desires in turn arise from an ego that is always grasping for more in an endless quest for self-assurance. For the Buddha, all such emotions have reasons and results; our task is to meditate upon them to understand how they rise and fall and thus be free from their power. He taught that applying such "scientific" thinking to oneself helps get rid of illusions and brings a new sense of clarity and self-control. Eventually one reaches a point at which the old sense of ego has disappeared, and one acts simply in response to situations as they arise, without any concern for gain. Done in such a state of mind, actions are spontaneous and natural, without any "load," so they do not create *reac*tions. Hence one breaks the cycle of cause and effect and becomes completely free. In other words, it is the intentions of action that cause its effects; if there are no selfish intentions, there are no effects.

In the Buddha's day most Indians believed (and still do) that all animals and humans live many lifetimes, not just one, with the form of each life shaped by how one lived in the last. Good living leads to a happy rebirth as a prosperous person or even a god; evil deeds lead to rebirth as a beggar or insect, usually after being punished in hell first. The Buddha accepted this idea, and made it part of his karma system of cause and effect. According to Buddhism, what we do now has effects that last beyond death to shape our next life, one way or another. For ordinary people, this means one should be compassionate and fair, to build up good karma for a better rebirth; for religious specialists, it means that if one meditates long enough one can reach a level at which one's actions leave no reactions or residues, and thus not be reborn any more at all but instead enter a state of perfect peace called **nirvana**. Nirvana is wonderful but cannot be defined and is not a place.

The Buddha traveled around northeastern India for about forty years after his **enlightenment**, preaching and instructing small groups of disciples. To ordinary people he taught a life of discipline, compassion, and devotion to spiritual leaders, but to his closest followers he taught a path of **meditation**, mind control, and intense discussion. It was through months and years of inward-looking, seated meditation that one could train the mind in the new way of seeing. Such meditation demanded a quiet lifestyle free of worries about money, success, and family, so the Buddha's disciples left their families, did not marry, and were forbidden to engage in business, farming, or military service. At first they followed the Buddha on his preaching tours, but eventually they settled down in small groups in villas or gardens donated to them by wealthy merchants who also admired the Buddha. During his lifetime the Buddha emphasized that his followers should test his teaching for themselves, not just believe what he said, so when he died there were a number of experienced disciples who could continue his message. Those who had "left the household life" lived in monasteries (for monks) and nunneries (for nuns) and devoted themselves to meditation and study, sharing the work of cleanup and repair, begging every day for food in nearby villages. They were not allowed to raise their own food, because such labor could distract them from meditation, and furthermore it involved killing insects and animals, which creates bad karma. Those who joined the monasteries gave up all they owned, took new religious names, and wore simple robes. At first the Buddha's teachings were recited orally to keep the memories alive, but eventually they were written down in books, which became Buddhist scriptures (called *sutras*).

The Buddha's teachings were eagerly received by many people in India because they seemed sensible and direct and did not involve elaborate and expensive sacrifices to the gods. They were adapted to individual needs, could be followed by anybody, and could be practiced anywhere, at home or on the road, if one were a traveling merchant. Within 150 years of the Buddha's death, his movement was well established in monasteries across northern India and began to move south to Ceylon (now Sri Lanka), east to what are now Burma and Thailand, and northwest toward modern Afghanistan. By the second century B.C., Buddhism was active in central Asia, particularly in oasis kingdoms along the main trade routes between India,

China, and the Mediterranean world. Wherever it went, Buddhism was accepted by many people as a new, liberating religion that had something for everybody; simple morality for peasants and sophisticated philosophy for intellectuals, all based on scriptural texts and interpreted by literate monks. As has happened with the founders of other religions, the Buddha came to be venerated as a superhuman being whose teaching was eternally true, even though one suspects such veneration would have made him uneasy.

Sometime in the first century A.D. the first Buddhist merchants from India or central Asia reached China, which controlled trade routes far to the west of its borders. By the next century there were Buddhist monks in several Chinese cities, preaching and translating scripture texts from Indian Sanskrit into Chinese. Many Chinese were interested; Buddhism offered some religious ideas and practices they had not known of before, such as karma and rebirth, hell or purgatory, meditation, monks and monasteries, and a well-developed philosophy of mind and knowledge. By this time Buddhists in India had images of the Buddha that they worshiped as symbols of his wisdom and compassion, using simple offerings of incense and fruit. Such images were also convenient objects of meditation, to remind meditators of who the Buddha was and what he had discovered. These images were also very popular in China, which had never seen anything like them before.

By the end of the second century A.D., there were several centers of Buddhism in China, and it grew rapidly from then on. The collapse of Han control made it easier for a foreign religion to get started, because people were more free to believe what they wanted. By the third century some aristocratic clans supported Buddhist missionaries and even produced a few young monks of their own. In 260 the first Chinese Buddhist pilgrim went to a kingdom in central Asia to study the faith and bring back scriptural texts to translate. He was the first of scores of such hardy pilgrims in the centuries to come, but early Chinese Buddhism depended heavily on monks from other lands who took the trouble to come to China and learn the language. The trip from India was very difficult and dangerous and could take as long as two years, so most of these missionaries never made it back home.

Buddhist thought was quite different from Chinese philosophy, so it took the Chinese a long time to understand it. Buddhism was more individualistic and psychological than the family-centered Chinese tradition, with its emphasis on agriculture, government, and a long, happy life in the midst of the world. But by the seventh century Chinese thinkers had developed forms of Buddhist philos-ophy and practice that fit the Chinese scene, the most important of which were **Pure Land** and **Chan** (which when it reached Japan later on was called Zen).

Buddhism Becomes Chinese: Pure Land and Chan/Zen

We have noted that Indian Buddhists came to regard the Buddha as a superhuman being whose teachngs are eternally true. Since they believed that every person had lived many lifetimes in different places, it was natural to believe that Sakyamuni had been through many life cycles before the rebirth in which he attained enlighten-ment. Some Indian thinkers had long maintained that our universe is just one of many, and that each universe has a history of birth, growth, and decline, a view quite similar to that of modern astron-omy. So it was that Buddhists began to say that in fact there were many Buddhas, one for each of the myriad universes, yet all preach-ing the same basic wisdom. As each universe went through cycles of death and rebirth, new Buddhas appeared to resume the teaching anew, because it too declined in power and had to be revived. Our world is the same; even now it is becoming more difficult to com-municate Sakyamuni's teaching because people are ignorant and stubborn, and a new Buddha-to-be—Maitreya, the future Bud-dha—(Chin. Mi-le Fo) is waiting in heaven to come to earth and start Buddhism all over again.

The combination of these ideas led to the belief that even in our universe there are many Buddhas, each in his own land or realm, each representing a particular Buddhist virtue, such as wisdom or compassion. Though Sakyamuni is the Buddha of our particular historical cycle, these other celestial Buddhas are available to help reinforce his teaching. The most popular of them is **Amitabha**, the Buddha of compassion (Chin. E-mi-tuo Fo) who presides over a paradise, or "Pure Land," (Chin. Jing-tu) far to the west. Those who believe in him, meditate upon him, and pray for his aid will be saved and go to his paradise at death. There they will be surrounded by the Buddha's influence and teaching and easily attain enlightenment. This belief was appealing to many people because it promised a better afterlife than going to purgatory or just being reborn on earth. It was also more specific than nirvana and gave people more to look forward to.

Indian scriptures describing Amitabha's paradise were translated into Chinese by the third century A.D., and by the sixth century some Chinese monks began to base their whole message on this belief, telling people that if they just called out Amitabha's name in faith they would be saved. There was no need for meditation or studying philosophy, or even being able to read; just faith and devotion were enough. These Buddhist evangelists went around preaching and organizing groups of Amitabha worshipers, and people responded by the tens of thousands. By the seventh century Pure Land was the most popular form of Buddhism in China, and it remains so to this day, in both China and Japan (which it reached in the ninth century). The appeal of this hope for paradise is easy to understand, because the Pure Land is described in Buddhist scriptures as a wonderful place indeed. In one book the Buddha tells his disciple Ananda that the Pure Land (Sukhavati in Sanskrit), is

the world system of the Lord Amitabha, rich and prosperous, comfortable, fertile, delightful and crowded with many Gods and men. And in this world system, Ananda, there are no hells, no animals, no ghosts, no Asuras [demons] and none of the inauspicious places of rebirth.

. . .

And that world system Sukhavati, Ananda, emits many fragrant odours, it is rich in a great variety of flowers and fruits, adorned with jewel trees, which are frequented by flocks of various birds with sweet voices. . . . And these jewel trees, Ananda, have various colours, many colours, many hundreds of thousands of colours. They are variously composed of the seven precious things, in varying combinations, i.e., of gold, silver, beryl, crystal, coral, red pearls or emerald.

. . .

And many kinds of river flow along in this world system Sukhavati. There are great rivers there, one mile broad, and up to fifty miles broad and twelve miles deep. And all these rivers flow along calmly, their water is fragrant with manifold agreeable odours, in them there are bunches of flowers to which various jewels adhere, and they resound with various sweet sounds.

In this paradise people get whatever they wish for, be it music, fine food, clothing, jewels, or palaces. They look and live like gods. But most important, in the Pure Land they constantly hear the Buddha's teaching, so that it is easy for them to attain enlightenment, never more to be reborn on earth. Believers are assured that nowhere in this wonderful place

does one hear of anything unwholesome, nowhere of the hindrances, nowhere of the states of punishment, the states of woe and the bad destinies, nowhere of suffering. Even of feelings which are neither pleasant nor unpleasant one does not hear here, how much less of suffering! And that, Ananda, is the reason why this world-system is called the "Happy Land" [Sukhavati].[7]

All this is available to those who sincerely believe in the Buddha and his power.

Pure Land Buddhism was fine for ordinary people, but it became a mass movement that some of the more individualistic and intellectual did not respond to. They were concerned for enlightenment now in this life and argued that however beautiful a Pure Land was, it was still not nirvana, the ultimate peace and clarity of mind. Some of them also felt that by the seventh and eight centuries (in the Tang period) Buddhism had become *too* successful. There were thousands of monasteries, many of them wealthy, with lots of land, servants, and golden images donated by rich merchants and officials. By this time there had been several Buddhist emperors who gave money and official status to monasteries and expected the monks to support them in return. Buddhism was becoming a new form of Chinese state religion, which some more dedicated monks thought distracted people from the real point of their faith: finding a new level of awareness and acceptance within. By the seventh century some reforming monks began a movement back to quiet meditation as the central practice of Buddhism. Before long, these monks were considered to be the founders of a new school of Buddhism, the meditation school, or *Chan*, a word that in Japanese is pronounced *"Zen."* This school soon became quite popular among pious officials and merchants, but it never had the mass appeal of Pure Land, because the Chan path to salvation took more time and hard work. In part it was a return to the self-enlightenment that had been advocated by Sakyamuni himself a thousand years earlier. Some Chan leaders, feeling that Buddhism had become too worldy and materialistic, rejected images and scriptures and spent their lives meditating in small isolated monasteries, but most Chan people felt that images and scriptures were useful reminders of Buddhist truth as long as one did not become attached to them and remembered that the potential for enlightenment was inside every person. Their slogan was "Become a Buddha yourself by realizing your own inner potential" (*Jian-xing cheng-fo*). It is not surprising that it is this form of Buddhism that has had the most appeal in North America and Europe, because it sounds similar to our own ideas of self-development. Listen, for example, to some passages from the teachings of the Chan masters:

> Within your own natures the ten thousand things will all appear, for all things of themselves are within your own natures. Given a name, this is the pure . . . Buddha.
>
> . . .
>
> Good friends, when I say "I vow to save all sentient beings everywhere," it is not that I will save you, but that sentient beings, each with their own natures, must save themselves. What is meant by "saving yourselves with your own natures"? Despite heterodox views, passions, ignorance, and delusions, in your own physical bodies you have in yourselves the attributes of inherent enlightenment, so that with correct views you can be saved. If you are awakened to correct views, the wisdom of *prajna* will wipe away ignorance and delusion and you all will save yourselves.
>
> . . .
>
> Good friends, each of you must observe well for himself. Do not mistakenly use your minds! The sutras say to take refuge in the Buddha within yourselves; they do not say to rely on other Buddhas. If you do not rely upon your own natures, there is nothing else on which to rely.[8]

Prajna is a Sanskrit term for the wisdom of the enlightened mind, which sees things as they really are, without fear or illusion. It is this wisdom that makes a Buddha a Buddha; since we can also attain such enlightenment, we can become Buddhas too. All the potential for salvation is in our own minds.

Even though various forms of Buddhism became very popular during the Tang dynasty, there were always some Daoists and Confucians who did not like it and who several times convinced rulers to make Buddhism illegal, confiscate monasteries, and force monks and nuns to return home. Most of these persecutions did not last long, but finally, in A.D. 844–845, a Daoist emperor forced thousands of monasteries to close and made most of the monks and nuns give up their religious vocations. This suppression of Buddhism was the most devastating of all. Then as now the Chinese government claimed complete authority over religion as well as politics and society. As a result of this nationwide persecution, many of the most important monasteries were ruined, and, with them, the schools of Buddhist study and philosophy they supported. Eventually the law was changed again, and Buddhism was allowed to rebuild, but now there were only two schools left, Chan and Pure Land, both of which survived because of their popular support. Since then, they have been the dominant forms of Buddhism in all of east Asia. The most important reason for their success in China is that they both were developed there by Chinese monks who knew what their people wanted—a religious hope that was simple, direct, and practical, and that in the case of Pure Land could be carried out in the midst of ordinary social life. Even Chan monks developed forms of meditation that could be practiced by merchants and officials at home. Chan leaders also taught that the eternal truth of Buddhism was the same as the cosmic Dao, so that one could seek enlightenment amid the beauties of nature. So it was that Buddhism too found its place in the Chinese view of the world.

A Revival of Confucianism

During the Han dynasty Confucianism became the official state philosophy; so when the Han dynasty fell, Confucianism lost prestige with it. After A.D. 220 it continued to exist as a conservative moral and social tradition but no longer produced many philosophers. For several hundred years the best philosophers in China were Buddhists, not Confucians. But eventually a reaction set in: Some officials and scholars began to worry that China was going to become so Buddhist that it would forget its own customs and culture, so they wrote articles and pamphlets attacking Buddhism as a foreign religion that the old Chinese sages had never heard of. By the eleventh century a few thinkers started to put together a new form of Confucian philosophy that was intended to provide a theoretical basis for all of life, from individual enlightenment to ruling the country. In so doing they borrowed ideas from Daoism and Buddhism, but combined them in a new system dominated by Confucian values, with Confucius venerated as wisest of all. The best known of these new Confucians was **Zhu Xi (Chu Hsi**, 1130–1200), who taught that everything in the world is composed of "vital substance" (qi), which is shaped into different forms according to "ordering principle" (li). Though at one level every type of thing has its own ordering principle, at a higher level all things are united by the supreme ordering principle of the whole universe, which Zhu Xi called the *tai-ji*, "the great ultimate." Of course, human beings are put together in this same way, though for most their qi is so dark and thick that it obscures their li. That is, their physical needs and psychological desires block their potential for intelligence and moral concern. To become better people they must meditate on the ordering principle within themselves and in the world around them, so that they gradually become more mature, rational, and in control of themselves. Li are patterns that make sense of life; these patterns should be discerned in Confucian books, in society and government, and in nature. Wherever one finds harmony and order, there are principles that can be understood and followed, such as loyalty between friends, the fairness and honesty of a good judge, or the structure and flexibility of a stalk of bamboo, which keeps springing back no matter how hard the wind blows. When one has studied and thought long enough on such things, li is strengthened and one eventually becomes a wise and mature person who can help bring order to family, society, and government.

This combination of individual development with social responsibility appealed to many people who thought that even Chan and Pure Land Buddhism still placed too much emphasis on finding salvation outside the ordinary world in a monastery or paradise. The government liked the new Confucianism too, because it affirmed that the existing social system would be fine as long as everyone lived according to the li of his or her position, for example, wife, father, or official. The principles of these social rules involved obedience to superiors, which, of course, was approved of by an authoritarian government. In the fourteenth century the government ordered that Zhu Xi's interpretations of the Confucian classics become the basis of civil service examination questions, so from then on every educated person had to study them.

Zhu Xi accepted ancestor worship and the veneration of the spirits of Chinese heroes, but he was opposed to Daoism, Buddhism, and the gods of popular religion and specifically denied that there was a supreme creator deity. The world simply came into existence through the interaction of li and qi, which are impersonal natural forces. This meant that after the new Confucianism was established many educated people became more skeptical about religion, or at least certain kinds of more personal and emotional religion. So it was that in China the religion of ordinary people had to develop on its own, without much help from intellectuals like the theologians of Christianity and Judaism. In China there was training for Buddhist monks and Daoist priests, but there were no seminaries that taught them to go out and preach to the people in a rational and orthodox

Temple of popular religion.

way, and indeed, there were no churches for people to go to. So, though the Chinese have always practiced some forms of religion and divination, for the past thousand years religious thought and institutions in China have not had the same high profile they have had in Europe and North America. Religion has been more a part of ordinary life and always ultimately under government control.

Popular Religion

Nevertheless, even if some intellectuals did not place much emphasis on religion, various kinds of rituals and beliefs continued to be important for the vast majority of the population. As far back as the records go, we read of a variety of religious activities practiced by all except a few of the more strict scholars, priests, and monks, including ancestor worship, sacrifices to spirits of sacred objects and places, belief in ghosts and demons, **exorcism**, divination, and the use of spirit-mediums. By the eleventh century (Song period) these practices had been blended together with Buddhist ideas of karma and rebirth and Daoist teachings about many levels of gods to form the popular religious system common from then on. Chinese popular religion is carried out in the midst of ordinary social life, in family, village, and city neighborhoods. It has no full-time specialists but is led by people who have other jobs, such as a farmer who may serve on a temple managerial committee, or a mechanic who works as a spirit-medium at night. There are popular religious temples where the gods are believed to live, but they usually have no resident clergy, just a caretaker or two. They are run and paid for by local people, who hire Daoist priests or Buddhist monks to perform special rituals. Worship in these temples is by individuals or families in the area who bring food offerings and incense to pray for blessings whenever they feel the need, though most come on the first or fifteenth of the lunar month or on festival days. In such temples there are no congregations or group worship, and usually no reciting of scriptures. In any event, most popular rituals are done at home before the family altar or at the shrine of the locality god who is responsible just for one field or neighborhood.

The gods of popular religion are almost all the spirits of former human beings who have been deified, unlike the star gods of

Daoism or the natural powers worshiped in the state religion. Since these gods were once human, they understand the needs of their worshipers, and furthermore they need their offerings and recognition if they are to keep their position as gods. Under Daoist influence popular gods were organized into a system like offices in a bureaucracy, each responsible for a specific function, such as healing smallpox, bringing children, or protecting fishermen. This system is ruled by the **Jade Emperor** in heaven, parallel to the emperor on earth. The Jade Emperor appoints the spirits of virtuous people to divine offices, which they hold temporarily until they are promoted for doing well or demoted for not being effective. In fact, if people feel their prayers are not being answered, they can abandon a god, or even a temple, and look for aid somewhere else. The offices remain much the same, but gods to fill them appear and disappear.

These gods are symbols of order, and many of them are believed to be equipped with weapons and celestial troops, as are some Daoist deities as well. Such force is necessary because beneath the gods is a vast array of demons, hostile influences that bring disease, suffering, and death—in a word, disorder. Ultimately the gods are more powerful, but these demons are violent and unruly and can be subdued only through repeated commands and dramatic rituals of exorcism. Most demons, or *gui*, are the spirits of the restless dead who died unjustly or whose bodies are not properly cared for; they cause disruption in order to draw attention to their problems. Other demons represent natural forces that can be dangerous, such as mountains and wild animals. Since these harmful spirits are believed to cause most illnesses, fires, and destructive weather, much effort is devoted to keeping them under control. A common method for driving them away is for a spirit-medium or Daoist priest to write out a charm in the name of a powerful god, a charm that is really a command such as might be issued by an emperor. Such a charm says something like, "I, the Jade Emperor, hereby order the evil and crooked forces causing this illness to leave immediately. This order has the power to smash and drive away all demons." The priest reads the charm aloud, then burns it so that its message is communicated to the sky through the smoke. There is a dramatic split in popular religion between the forces of good and evil.

*Women reading scriptures
and praying at a popular
temple.*

Most people in China had to struggle just to survive every day, so
they easily felt threatened and did all they could to fight back,
from working hard in their fields and protesting against unfair
landlords to hiring a spirit-medium to heal a daughter's fever. This
spirit of struggle has a lot to do with the success of Chinese people
today.

There is another kind of Chinese popular religion, organized as
sects or denominations similar to Protestant Christian groups in
North America and Europe that are led and supported by ordinary
people. These sects, still active in Taiwan, have their own books of
scripture, which they chant or sing from in group worship. People
join these associations as individuals looking for their own religious satisfaction, whereas in general popular religion there are no
members, just families who worship in a village temple because
they happen to live there. The sects go back in Chinese history to

groups like the Yellow Turbans at the end of the Han dynasty, but they took their present shape in the thirteenth century under Buddhist influence. Some evangelistic monks started organizing groups of followers outside the monasteries, teaching them Buddhist beliefs in simple form, mostly about Amitabha's paradise. These groups grew so rapidly that more conservative monks became jealous and reported them to the government, which outlawed them because it was uneasy about any organized associations among the people. Once the sects were declared illegal, it was difficult for orthodox monks to work with them, so they were left on their own. They picked up a lot of ideas from Daoism and popular religion and tried to protect themselves by forming communes to raise their own food. When they were attacked by police or troops, some of them resisted with weapons, and even raided towns themselves; the government considered them just bandits or rebels. Perhaps because of this pressure, some sects started emphasizing Maitreya, the future Buddha, whom they said was coming soon to bring in a new world where they would be safe and happy. In the fourteenth century a few sects rebelled against the Mongols in the name of Maitreya, which confirmed their bad reputation with the government.

However, for the most part, the sects were peaceful and provided a way for some people to be more religious if they wanted to be and go directly to paradise at death, without going through purgatory first. By the sixteenth century the beliefs of most of these groups were centered on a great mother goddess who created the world and humankind and loves everybody as her own children. Unfortunately her children have forgotten the Mother, their real parent, and where they came from, and so they lead sinful lives and get into trouble because of sex, drinking, dishonesty, and stealing. Sectarian scriptures were regarded as having been revealed by the Mother or her messengers to remind people of who they are, how they should live, and how they can be saved. Those who believe the message should join the sect and share the good news with others. These scriptures were passed on from one sect leader to the next and used as the basis of preaching, ritual, and discussion. Sect members were supposed to be more pious and good than their neighbors; their perception of themselves was very different from that of the government.

Foreign Religions in China Besides Buddhism

During the Tang dynasty China was again open to trade with foreign countries, so there was opportunity for foreign religions to come as well. In the seventh century some Christians reached China from what is now Syria, and many thousands more came in the thirteenth century during the period of Mongol rule. These Christians, called Nestorians after the name of the founder of their denomination, built churches in several Chinese cities and at one point had up to thirty thousand members, but for the most part their members were non-Chinese who had been brought in by the Mongols to help with administration and trade. They disappeared when the Mongols and other foreigners were driven out in the fourteenth century. There were a few Italian Catholic missionaries in China during the thirteenth and fourteenth centuries who also built churches, but their work too disappeared without a trace. The third time Christians tried to gain a foothold in China they were more successful, due primarily to the work of Italian Jesuits who arrived in the sixteenth century. They were intelligent and well educated, learned Chinese, and eventually were given permission to preach and build churches. By that time European astronomy and mathematics were superior to Chinese (though this was not true earlier), so a few of the Jesuits were appointed as court astronomers and mathematicians in Beijing. The Jesuits did a good job of communicating Christian teaching in language aristocratic Chinese could understand, though they played down Jesus' miracles and crucifixion. They accepted ancestor worship and agreed that Confucius was a very wise man. Before long, other Roman Catholic missionaries were admitted to China as well, and the church grew rapidly. However, some of the more conservative priests thought Jesuit attitudes went too far toward ancestors and Confucius, and they complained to the pope. After several decades of debate, a pope ordered the Jesuits to change their approach and forbid ancestor worship, which disgusted the Chinese, so they sent a lot of missionaries home and closed their churches. It was made illegal for Chinese to become Christians, but some did anyway; although the church was weakened it still survived. When a new wave of Roman Catholic missionaries came to China after 1840, they found several thousand Chinese Christians already there, but just a handful of priests.

A few Protestant missionaries from Europe and America first came to China in the early nineteenth century, and many more were permitted to come as a result of the treaties the Chinese were forced to sign when they lost wars with Britain and France. The Protestants translated the Bible into everyday spoken Chinese, brought in modern printing presses, and established schools and hospitals as well as churches, so they had an important impact on Chinese culture. However, not many Chinese actually became Christians, a pattern that continued into the twentieth century. Before 1949 Chinese Christian churches were still heavily dependent on foreign missionaries and financial support.

The other major foreign religion in China is Islam, which was brought there by Arab and central Asian Muslims in the eighth century. Many more Muslims came during the Mongol period, when China was wide open to the rest of the world, and settled in cities all over the country, but mostly in the western provinces. There are now about 30 million Muslims in China, more than in Saudi Arabia. Though they have intermarried with other Chinese, they have kept their religion and taught their children Arabic so they can read the Qur'an (Koran), the holy book of Islam.

Before the new wave of Christian missionaries in the nineteenth century, the only foreign religion to have much impact on Chinese culture was Buddhism. By contrast, Islam has always been the religion of a large central Asian immigrant group, and earlier Christian efforts failed to have much impact on the life of China, and even more recent Christian missionary work did not convert more than a few million Chinese in a huge population. The relative lack of success of these foreign religions in converting large numbers of Chinese is an indication of how Chinese culture has continued to be tough and self-contained.

CHAPTER III

Types of Beliefs and Activities in Chinese Religious Life

Though there is great variety in the religions of the world, they all share common themes, activities, and concerns that make it easier for us to compare and understand them. Every religion has some basic understanding of the world and how it came to be, and has certain places, persons, and actions it considers supremely important or sacred. Now that we have looked briefly at the historical development of Chinese religions, it might help to see how some of these basic unifying types of belief and activity were understood in China, always keeping our own experience and culture in mind as a basis for comparison. Every religion believes that its teachings are special and reveal basic truths about life and the world. Our task is neither to dispute nor to support these claims, but to try to understand them in as objective and balanced a way as we can. After we have understood, then we are free as individuals to agree or criticize, choose, reject, or enjoy. One more thing to remember: living religion is as much what people do as what they think, so in this chapter we will discuss rituals, buildings, and types of leaders as well as beliefs.

World View

In Chapter I we have already discussed the traditional Chinese understanding of how the world is and came to be. Such an understanding is a set of basic assumptions about the origins and nature of life. These assumptions shape everything else people do or say. The following are two famous statements of the Chinese world view by Confucian philosophers of the eleventh century A.D., Zhang Zai (1020–1077) and Zhou Dun-yi (1017–1073):[9]

Heaven is my father and Earth is my mother, and even such a small creature as I find an intimate place in their midst.

Therefore that which fills the universe I regard as my body and that which directs the universe I consider as my nature.

All people are my brothers and sisters, and all things are my companions.

The great ruler (the emperor) is the eldest son of my parents (Heaven and Earth), and the great ministers are his stewards. Respect the aged—this is the way to treat them as elders should be treated. Show deep love toward the orphaned and the weak—this is the way to treat them as the young should be treated. The sage identifies his character with that of Heaven and Earth, and the worthy is the most outstanding man. Even those who are tired, infirm, crippled, or sick; those who have no brothers or children, wives or husbands, are all my brothers who are in distress and have no one to turn to.

Zhang Zai, "The Western Inscription"

The Ultimate of Non-being and also the Great Ultimate (Tai-ji)! The Great Ultimate through movement generates *yang*. When its activity reaches its limit, it becomes tranquil. Through tranquility the Great Ultimate generates *yin*. When tranquility reaches its limit, activity begins again. So movement and tranquility alternate and become the root of each other, giving rise to the distinction of *yin* and *yang*, and the two modes are thus established.

By the transformation of *yang* and its union with *yin*, the Five Agents of Water, Fire, Wood, Metal, and Earth arise. When these five material forces [qi] are distributed in harmonious order, the four seasons run their course.

The Five Agents constitute one system of *yin* and *yang*, and *yin* and *yang* constitute one Great Ultimate. The Great Ultimate is fundamentally the Non-ultimate. The Five Agents arise, each with its specific nature.

When the reality of the Ultimate of Non-being and the essence of *yin*, *yang*, and the Five Agents come into mysterious union, integration ensues. *Qian* (Heaven) constitutes the male element, and *kun* (Earth) constitutes the female element. The interaction of these two material forces engenders and transforms the myriad things. The myriad things produce and reproduce, resulting in an unending transformation.

It is man alone who receives (the Five Agents) in their highest excellence, and therefore he is most intelligent. His physical form appears, and his spirit develops consciousness. The five moral principles of his nature (humanity or *ren*, righteousness, propriety, wisdom, and faithfulness) are aroused by, and react to, the external world and engage in activity; good and evil are distinguished; and human affairs take place.

Zhou Dun-yi, "An Explanation of the Diagram
of The Great Ultimate"

These statements mean that the world came into being through natural processes, and that everything we know of is part of this universe and therefore related to all the other parts. This includes human beings and gods as well; we are all united in one big system, with nothing outside it. There are some creation stories in China, but in them the basic physical stuff of the world already exists at the beginning; the gods or culture heroes just organize it into the forms we know. This view of the world is similar to that of many other cultures, such as the Hopi or the Sioux in North America, but it is quite different from the traditional teachings of Judaism, Christianity, and Islam. In these religions there is just one God, who exists outside the world, which he then decides to create. Here, it is really God that is sacred, not the world itself. The Chinese approach tends to give more religious meaning to life in the midst of the world, and does not emphasize a higher spiritual reality that individuals should try to attain. Of course there are high level symbols in China like Tian and the Daoist star gods, and, on the other hand, in Christianity, Jesus Christ is a symbol of God's involvement with the world, but the basic difference between the two world views is still clear. In each case the tradition is shaped by its fundamental understanding of reality.

Sacred Space

Most people have a sense of special places where their lives have been shaped and changed; homes, schools, neighborhoods, mountains, or woods. As we grow older we may go back to visit these places; it is comforting to find houses, shops, or beaches as they were, and a bit upsetting to find them gone or covered by a new shopping center. Nations and towns also have places that remind them of their founders and heroes, like the Lincoln Memorial in Washington, the Parliament buildings in Ottawa, or a battlefield in Princeton, New Jersey, where the Americans defeated the British in the Revolutionary War.

Religions have special places too, where people believe the real truth of things has been revealed, like certain churches, synagogues, shrines to saints, or towns where the founder lived, like Mecca and Bethlehem. Worshipers visit such places regularly to be reminded of who they are and to be inspired to do better.

In China, as in native American religions, the world itself is a sacred place, so the Chinese have always understood their world to be full of holy mountains, caves, and landscapes that particularly reveal the power and beauty of the earth. Even today Chinese vacationers go in groups to visit beauty spots, especially those that have been praised by a poet or painter. Daoism and the state religion organized China's geography into areas controlled by sacred mountains. Shrines and altars were built on these mountains where sacrifices were offered to petition for rain. The landscape was organized into smaller areas as well, with a locality god (earth god) for each neighborhood or field and city gods for county-seat towns. Lower in status than the locality gods were deities of the household bed, kitchen, and doorway, each with a little niche for a paper image and incense.

Buddhist monasteries and the temples of Daoism and popular religion provided parallel sacred places, as did little shrines along the roadsides for the spirits of the dead who, because they had died violently, were believed to have special powers. People regularly visited these places to ask for healing or for children, or to report deaths and weddings to the gods; some people in Taiwan and Hong Kong, and even in parts of rural China, still do. In China the whole world was potentially sacred, from crossroads, wells, and old trees to the highest mountain ranges. The most direct evidence for this is the feng-shui discussed in Chapter I. Feng-shui assumes that the earth is alive with lines of force; those living where such lines come together will have vitality and good fortune. People in Hong Kong may have no choice in the location and orientation of their apartments, but many of them still arrange their furniture on feng-shui principles, with a sofa facing south along a north wall or a cabinet set to block potentially hostile lines of force from across the street. The result can be a pleasant arrangement satisfying both religion and art.

Sacred Time

Special places go with special times, for both individuals and groups. For individuals there are birthdays, graduations, and promotions; for families, Christmas and summer holidays; annual parades and fairs for towns. These are all times of remembering the past and renewing togetherness, times when we break regular routines to relax, when executives or workers are just people enjoying themselves. There are similar days for whole nations, such as the Fourth of July, Canada Day, and Thanksgiving.

Because of the well-known Chinese emphasis on the family and group, individual celebrations were not so important as they are for us. The birth of a male child was a cause for rejoicing, but there were no religious rituals associated with it, and not much attention was paid to individual birthdays until one reached sixty. The real birthday for everyone was New Year's Day, when the powers of cosmic life were renewed and everyone was counted a year older. The most important celebrations in a lifetime were at marriage and death, but even then family interests were central. Marriage was essentially a contract between two families, arranged by the parents through professional "go-betweens." The wishes of the couple involved had little influence; they were often betrothed to each other when they were small children, and may not have seen each other before the wedding. Marriage rituals consisted of exchange of gifts and agreements between the families, culminating in a great feast at the groom's home on the day the bride was brought there in a sedan chair, together with her furniture for the new family unit at her in-laws' house. No priests were involved, no exchange of vows by the couple.

Hired dancers in a funeral procession.

The Chinese equivalent was introducing the bride and groom to each other's families. The first time the couple was alone was in their bedroom at the end of the first wedding day (the whole process took about three days). Rituals we might call religious were involved with marriage at only two points, the first before betrothal when a diviner was consulted to see if the horoscopes of the couple were compatible. The second point was on the first wedding day; when the bride first entered the groom's house they both bowed briefly before the tablets of his ancestors.

Funeral rituals were very complex and took days to complete. Their essential point was to prepare a peaceful afterlife for the deceased, and ensure that he or she would become a cooperative ancestral spirit who could help the family later on. The rituals included placing the open coffin in the main room of the house, offering food to the spirit of the dead, praying to the gods for safe passage to the underworld, and a procession to the grave, with sedan chairs, orchestra, and mourners wearing sackcloth. At the grave site, chosen through feng-shui, there was a ritual to place the spirit in its ancestral tablet, followed by a last ceremonial feast. After the coffin was buried the family returned home with the tablet, placed it on the

family altar, and inaugurated it with a second feast, some of which
was brought back from the tomb. Death was accepted, but the real
emphasis in funeral rituals was on strengthening the continuing life
of the family, through such practices as throwing beans and nails on
the bottom of the coffin to symbolize a desire for many sons. (The
word for nail is *ding*, pronounced the same as another character
meaning male person.)

Centuries ago there were initiation rites for young men and wom-
en in China, consisting essentially of giving a new adult name and
cap to a man, and giving a special hair-do and new clothes to a
woman. Over the years, however, these rites came to be celebrated
just before marriage, which was the real coming of age as a produc-
ing member of society. It is interesting to realize that in China what
we now think of as individual celebrations were primarily devoted to
the well-being of the group. This has a lot to do with the sense of
mutual dependence and relatedness that characterized the Chinese

*A woman offering incense
at a popular temple.*

view of life. Of course, in the old days European weddings and funerals were more family-oriented too, and most marriages were arranged by parents or at least only with their consent.

All religions, too, have times they remember as special occasions
of power and revelation for the group, like Easter or Yom Kippur;
there are usually such "holy days" for every season of the year, and
for saints and founders as well. Religion in China is no exception;
there are festivals throughout the year, from New Year's to the winter solstice. There were no weeks or weekends in old China, so these
festivals had economic functions as well as religious and social ones;
they gave people time off from work, time to be with family and
friends and to eat good food. For the poor, festivals could be the
only days they ate meat.

The most important annual festival is New Year's, which is celebrated for over a month. According to traditional customs the festival begins in (our) December with a ritual to send the household
gods to heaven, where they report on family activities during the
preceding year. Then the house is cleaned to get rid of old dirt and
bad influences, to start the new year fresh. Debts are paid off for the
same reason. On the last night of the year, families gather for a big
feast, which is first offered to the spirits of the ancestors, who are
believed to eat the invisible essence of the food. The house is sealed
to keep out the last old qi of the year, and the family stays awake all
night, talking and playing games, with everyone being sure to mention only good things and not say words that sound like those for
death and disease. What one does that night influences good or bad
fortune for the whole year, a bit like our New Year's resolutions,
only more so. At dawn the doors are opened to let in the powerful,
fresh, vital breath of the new year. The household gods are wel-
comed back with new paper images, and the oldest man in the family offers food and incense outdoors to the gods in heaven. During
the next few days people visit each other with gifts of money or food,
make offerings at local temples, and watch parades of paper lions
and dragons. In China, New Year's Day is also everyone's birthday
(though people have individual birthdays too), which further con-
tributes to a strong sense of starting afresh.

In the spring there is the Pure and Bright (Qing-ming) Festival,
one hundred six days after the winter solstice, in early April. The
Spring Festival began as a kind of continuation of the New Year's

Festival, so it emphasized the importance of taking baths in flowing streams to wash away the dirt, disease, and harmful forces that had accumulated in the previous year. Closely related to this washing was the "Cold Food Festival" for the renewal of fire, celebrated at about the same time. All old fires were put out for three days, while people ate cold food that had been prepared beforehand. At the end of this period, new fires were started in the ancient way, by rubbing sticks together, to symbolize the rebirth of yang power in the new spring season.

One theme in the old Spring Festival was worship of ancestors, and as time passed this element became more and more important; eventually the festival became a time of honoring the family dead by cleaning their graves and offering food to their spirits as part of a big picnic. In this way the dead are reintegrated into the life of the family, making the Spring Festival a time of both sadness and joy. It reminds one a bit of Easter in Christian communities. (There is a detailed description of a Spring Festival ritual picnic in the next chapter).

Another exciting time for people in old China was the Midsummer Festival, celebrated on the fifth day of the fifth lunar month at the summer solstice, the longest day of the year. On this day, the power of yang has reached its peak, and the power of yin is about to be reborn. People were ambivalent about this. On the one hand, too much of anything is bad, so one did not want to do things that encouraged yang any more. Hence, no big fires were lit, and boys born during this time were considered potentially dangerous. (Boys usually have enough yang already; too much will make them too aggressive). On the other hand, the revival of yin leads eventually to the cold and darkness of winter. Yin was associated with disease, death, and demons; at the midsummer festival, people went up into the hills to collect medicinal herbs to ward off disease. The power of such herbs comes from yang, so this is the time they are most charged with the ability to hold off yin diseases. People also hung up protective charms at this time, made of yang symbols like red paper and peachwood.

The other major festival of the Chinese sacred year is the Feast of Souls on the fifteenth of the seventh lunar month (late August). This festival is influenced by Buddhist ideas of purgatory and rebirth. Purgatory is a place where the souls of the dead go to be purged (cleansed) of their sins before they are reborn in a new life. The Chinese believe that such souls need help from their living relatives, so pious and responsible families have Buddhist monks read scriptures and burn incense to encourage the souls as they are being punished for their sins in one compartment of purgatory after the next.

However, there are many lost souls in purgatory with no families to pray for them, and Buddhist compassion demands that these desperate, hungry souls be cared for as well. The belief developed that in the seventh lunar month the gates of purgatory open for a time, and all the lost souls can fly back to earth to receive food offerings and hear scriptures read for their salvation. So the Feast of Souls is a time of rituals for the dead, both by individual families and in temples and monasteries. For their own relatives, Buddhist families sometimes have monks burn elaborate paper houses full of paper furniture, food, and ritual money, all to be transferred to purgatory through the flames for the comfort of the dead.

The Chinese celebrate other festivals as well, such as a mid-autumn harvest festival in honor of the moon. At this time of year one can still buy moon-cakes in Chinese bakeries around the world.

Another type of festival is in honor of the birthday of the god in a local temple. Such birthday rituals involve hiring priests to recite scriptures and make offerings, entertaining gods and worshipers with popular operas on outdoor stages, and taking an image of the deity on a tour of its district to drive out harmful forces and renew good ones.

In religions all over the world there is a sense that sacred power periodically runs down and has to be renewed, just as personal energy needs to be recharged by sleep and vacations. For religion, this renewal takes place in rituals that are repeated every year or even every few days. In them, people recall the actions and words of their gods and heroes and resolve to do over again in their time what was once done long ago. In this way, religious meaning is made fresh again in the face of forgetting, indifference, and death.

Symbols of Superhuman Power

Our world is full of special people to whom we turn for inspiration and guidance; parents, teachers, ministers, athletes, musicians, movie stars—even some politicians! Younger people sometimes model their dress and actions on such heroes and stand in line all night just for the chance to see and hear a rock music star. Sometimes the popularity and lifestyle of such people are so far beyond our own that they seem to be another species of human being; they have much money and the freedom to buy what they want and go where they wish. Even though popular magazines tell us about their problems, it is easy to idolize such people, sometimes far beyond what they deserve. In addition, in the movies, there are beings with special knowledge and abilities, beings like Superman, Jedi knights, and space voyagers from other planets. All this tells us that many people still have a longing to know about extraspecial persons, even if only as entertainment.

At another level such longing is found in religion as well, though in religion special beings can be believed to be really superhuman, even gods themselves. Such gods can be symbols of everything we want to be or should be, or symbols of immortality or of wisdom and power far beyond our own. In religions familiar in North America and Europe there is a range of such figures, like Moses, Muhammed, Jesus Christ, and the God of the universe behind them all. We have already seen that there are Chinese parallels to these figures, many of them. In the Chinese world view there is not a sharp distinction between gods and humans; all are parts of the same system: Humans are potentially divine, and gods often take human form. People can live forever or even be resurrected from the dead if they know the correct rituals and alchemical drugs. So it is that most gods of popular religion are deified humans, venerated for their courage, strength, or compassion. The Buddhas too were once human, so they also can understand the needs of their worshipers. The cosmic gods of Daoism are provided with images and titles, and even mountains and rivers can respond to human pleas. After all, are not they too made of the same vital substance?

A good example of a popular Chinese deity is **Ma-zu (Ma-tsu)**, the goddess of fishermen and sailors, who is supposed to have begun her divine career as a pious young woman who lived on an island off the southern coast in the eleventh century A.D. This girl, who never married, was believed to be able to calm typhoons and to be able, while she was in a trance, to send out her spirit to rescue people drowning at sea. She died young, with lots of life energy left over and no husband or children to worship her restless spirit. Before long, local people began to worship her, claiming that their prayers had been answered, children healed, and fathers brought home from the sea. The spirit's fame spread and came to the attention of officials. Sailors on imperial naval expeditions turned to her for aid, and some claimed she had saved them from storms and pirates. On one such expedition, it was a crown prince who was saved, and when he became emperor, he had a temple built in her honor and gave her a new, more exalted title. In this way the girl became a goddess, with ever-widening fame and several titles, but she is popularly known today in Hong Kong as Tian-hou, "Queen of Heaven," and in Taiwan as Ma-zu, "Grandmother."

Here is a folktale about Ma-zu as a young girl that illustrates how she was understood by ordinary people:

Although the girl was only seven years old she already possessed supernatural powers. Her father and her two brothers were merchants, and each time they were overtaken by a storm during the sea crossing, she rescued them from the waves without anyone's being aware of it.

One day her father and brothers were once more on the sea when a terrific storm sprang up. She felt very troubled at their great danger, and her soul immediately left her body and hurried to their assistance. Being half immortal, she arrived in an instant at the sea, where the waves were breaking as high as the sky.

The ship was pitching and tossing in all directions, and the passengers, pale with terror, thought that their last hour had come. The daughter grasped her brothers in her arms and her father in her mouth and flew over the sea. It made no difference to her whether the sea was deep or shallow. The three castaways saw only a little girl appear through the winds and the waves to save them, and they thought that she was an immortal; they had no idea that she was their own little girl.

Before leaving she had been talking with her mother, who was frightened out of her wits when her daughter broke off in the middle of a word and her body became stiff and cold. The mother thought she had fallen ill, and began to sob and weep, but the girl lay as though she were dead.

After she had called and fondled her for a long time, the girl suddenly said, "Yes." "Wake up, child," said the mother, "I nearly wept myself to death." "Father is dead." "What are you saying?" cried the mother. "Father and my two brothers were overtaken by a terrible storm on the sea, and the ship sank, but my soul hastened over the water to save them. I grasped my brothers in my two hands, and caught my father's clothes in my mouth. But you wept and called for me, until my heart was touched, and I had to answer 'Yes,' whereupon my father dropped out of my mouth. I would otherwise have saved him, but immediately after his fall he was hidden by the waves, and I could find no trace of him. I managed to save my brothers, but, alas, father is dead!" "Is that really true?" asked the mother. "Yes." "Oh, woe is me, woe is me!"

Soon the brothers came home. Weeping, they clasped their mother in their arms and told her how first their father had been saved and later drowned. The daughter reproached her mother, saying, "You are to blame for the death of my father. Look, my feet and hair are still moist." The mother embraced her children again.

The daughter was sorry for her mother's widowed state and swore an oath never to marry. She tied her hair together and waited on her mother till her death. After her death she became an immortal. She became protectoress of merchants and ships on the rivers, and is particularly worshipped by them.[10]

Deities such as Ma-zu have special abilities and limited powers, but when linked together with other gods they are believed to be able to do just about anything a single, supreme god can, from helping an army win a battle to healing a sore on a child's neck. It is all a matter of knowing what temple to visit to meet one's needs. All the gods have names and life stories to help people know what they can do: a deified general for a son at war; an ancient physician for healing illness. Popular operas portray the gods on stage, so even illiterate people know who they are. Beliefs concerning some deities are based on hero stories in novels; others are discussed by storytellers and spirit-mediums.

Rituals: Actions That Relate Us To Divine Power

The basic theme of Chinese ritual is *reciprocity*: a mutual exchange of gifts and favors between gods and worshipers, so that both gain from the transaction. In China the most common way of forming a

Offering food at a popular temple.

reciprocal relationship is through sharing a meal; when guests eat, they recognize that they owe the host a favor. Most ritual offerings consist of food—cooked for gods and ancestors, uncooked for ghosts. Cooked food is usually left on an altar or table for a while until the gods have eaten its inner essence; then their worshipers take it home and eat it as food blessed with divine power, a Chinese form of Holy Communion. Food offerings are a shared meal; the god, as a guest, is expected to grant a favor in return, a favor requested through a prayer in the ritual. Chinese gods are treated with formality, particularly those in higher positions, and those honored in elaborate Daoist or state rituals. But even in Daoism, the priest is believed to have the powers of a god during ritual; after all, he has prepared himself for years and can call divine powers down upon himself. The Buddhist nun too knows that the Buddha image before her represents a potential for wisdom and compassion she has within herself. At the popular level, gods are treated as important guests, as divine officials, but nonetheless worshipers know that the gods need them too, so there can be a kind of familiarity in worship that is different from the solemnity of services in a Confucian temple or a Presbyterian church. There are some parallels between these Chinese deities and the saints of popular Roman Catholicism, who also represent special virtues and powers, easily available to their devotees.

In addition to ancestor worship, the oldest and most formal Chinese rituals that we know of in any detail are those of the state religion. One took place at the winter solstice, on the longest night of the year, when the dark force of yin is at its peak. The emperor and his officials rose before dawn to offer sacrifice to Heaven and the power of yang to support the rebirth of light and warmth in the middle of winter, to make sure that spring would come again. Dressed in an embroidered robe, the emperor climbed to the top of a great round stone altar south of the city, the direction of yang. There, officials called out to the royal ancestors and Heaven in a loud, slow monotone, asking for their aid and assuring them of the ruler's devoted support. The ancestors, and deities of the sun, moon, stars, planets, wind, and rain were represented by inscribed tablets. Food was offered before these tablets; soup, vegetables, and fruits, together with fish, beef, and pork. A young red bull without a blemish (a symbol of yang) was offered to Heaven. Its flesh was burned on a special altar. Wine, incense and silk were also presented, all accompanied by the music of bells and drums. If all went smoothly and well, and the weather was clear, the emperor was confident that he had done his part and that the ancestors and Heaven would do theirs as well. The spirit and intention of such rituals is well illustrated by prayers offered to the "Ruler on High" (Shang-di; in the following passage called Shang-te or Te) by the emperor. There is much in this prayer that sounds familiar to a Jew, Muslim, or Christian:

Of old in the beginning, there was the great chaos, without form and dark. The five elements had not begun to revolve, nor the sun and the moon to shine. In the midst thereof there existed neither form nor sound. Thou, O spiritual Sovereign, camest forth in Thy presidency, and first didst divide the grosser parts from the purer. Thou madest heaven; Thou madest earth; Thou madest man. All things with their re-producing power, got their being.

O Te, when Thou hadst separated the *Yin* and the *Yang* (i.e., the heavens and the earth), Thy creating work proceeded. Thou didst produce, O Spirit, the sun and the moon and the five planets, and pure and beautiful was their light. The vault of heaven was spread out like a curtain, and the square earth supported all on it, and all things were happy. I, Thy servant, venture reverently to thank Thee, and, while I worship, present the notice to Thee, O Te, calling Thee Sovereign.

Thou hast vouchsafed, O Te, to hear us, for Thou regardest us as a Father. I, Thy child, dull and unenlightened, am unable to show forth my dutiful feelings. I thank Thee, that Thou has accepted the intimation. Honourable is Thy great name. With reverence we spread out these gems and silks, and, as swallows rejoicing in the spring, praise Thine abundant love.

The great feast has been set forth, and the sound of our joy is like thunder. The Sovereign Spirit vouchsafes to enjoy our offering, and my heart feels within me like a particle of dust. The meat has been boiled in the large caldrons, and the fragrant provisions have been prepared. Enjoy the offering, O Te, then shall all the people have happiness. I, Thy servant, receiving Thy favours, am blessed indeed.[11]

The use of animal flesh in state rituals has continued in popular religion, but is prohibited in Buddhism and some branches of Daoism. Though there are sticks of incense and bowls of fruit on Buddhist altars, characteristic Buddhist rituals are more verbal and personal, with group readings of scripture, recitation of the names of Buddhas, and quiet prayers. Rituals performed by Daoist priests are the most elaborate of all, with clouds of incense smoke; a small orchestra of Chinese violins, clarinets, bells, and drums; stately dances; complex hand movements; and the chanting of invocations and commands. But despite their differences, all these rituals are united by a common theme: the forming of a temporary relationship with gods or Buddhas through offering them gifts of food and incense, along with a kind of ritual money used in popular religion. Such relationships oblige the gods to respond in some way, even though it may not be exactly the way the worshiper has in mind.

Of course, such reciprocity is expected by ordinary worshipers in all religions, though some theologians maintain that the proper attitude toward the highest gods is reverence with no expectation of reward. Underneath, most people feel that if they go to church and act decently, God should take care of them, and they complain if things go wrong. Popular religion in Western culture means expecting specific, positive answers to prayers before trips, operations, or football games. Here again, religious attitudes are a special form of ordinary social interaction, in which we assume that a favor done is a favor due. Society is built on mutual obligations, some of which we make into legal requirements, so it is not surprising to find religious rituals operating in the same way.

Divination and Exorcism

Most people would like to be able to anticipate the future, so they make plans, have medical examinations, invest their money, and listen to weather reports. Underneath something like a television weather report is the sense that foreknowledge gives us a certain degree of control over our lives; if there is a blizzard in Chicago we can decide to postpone our trip to New York, or to fly by way of Atlanta instead. Chinese religion is full of such concern to control the future, expressed at a much more intense level than most of us feel now. In the first place, there are many auspicious words in Chinese that are repeatedly invoked or written to bring about the promise they imply. Fancy rice bowls are inscribed with such phrases as *Wan-shou wu-jiang* "[May you have] ten thousand long lives with no limit," and such characters as *xi* ("joy") and *lu* ("good salary") are hung on walls on red paper scrolls or form designs on clothing. Symbolic puns are used as well, such as pictures of fish, pronounced *yu*, the same pronunciation as another character meaning "abundance."

In old China, and still today in Taiwan and Hong Kong, there were almanacs listing what was good or bad to do on every day of the year; people consulted such almanacs before they decided to do anything significant, from taking a trip to getting married. For more important events they also consulted fortune-tellers, who calculated their fate on the basis of which natural forces were strongest at their time of birth, as we saw in the feng-shui story in Chapter I. There were also specialists who predicted the future of individuals from the shape of their faces and the lines on their hands.

Divination was also carried out as part of temple rituals to determine how the gods would respond to offerings. After praying for aid, worshipers would throw wooden blocks on the floor in front of the altar, blocks shaped like half-moons, one side flat and the other round. A round and flat side up together is a yes answer to a prayer, because it expresses yin and yang in balance; the same sides up mean no. Another common method was to shake numbered, two-foot-long sticks out of a round canister. The first stick to fall out was taken to an attendant in a little booth at the side of the sanctuary, who matched its number with one of a row of paper slips hung on the wall behind him. Each slip had an obscure verse that the attendant read and interpreted to the worshiper as his or her fortune for the day.

The oldest form of divination was a more complex procedure based on reading the significance of sets of six horizontal lines, broken and unbroken. These sets, called hexagrams in English, were formed by sorting out fifty dried plant stalks, with certain numerical values assigned to groups of stalks, values corresponding to types of lines, which were written down one at a time as the stalks were counted off. The whole process was controlled except at one point; the first random division of the bunch of stalks into two. The Chinese believed that at that point one's existence was partially open to cosmic influence, so the rest of the process was the spelling out of what one's destiny was at that moment.

Chinese archaeologists have recently discovered similar sets of lines on prehistoric pottery, so this form of divination is very old indeed. Over the centuries traditions developed about the significance of lines and hexagrams, which were understood to include different mixes of the two basic forces of life, the male which initiates and the female which completes, like *yang* and *yin*, represented respectively by solid and broken lines, ———— and —— ——. Specialists in line divination tried to include every possible life situation in the six-line sets, so that eventually there were sixty-four hexagrams, composed of eight different groups of three lines (trigrams). Each hexagram was assigned a certain meaning, ranging between good fortune and bad fortune, or a mix of the two, depending on the circumstances. So, for example, the hexagram *fu* (returning) is a good sign because it portrays the rebirth of *yang* power coming up from below, just when it seemed that the dark forces of *yin* had taken over.

— —
— —
— —
— —
— —
———

This is what the commentary says about *fu*:
Returning. Good fortune
One can go out and come in without distress
. . .
There is advantage in having a place to go.

From this one can see that *fu* is a positive and encouraging indication. One meditating on it could get a fresh perspective on an important decision, such as whether to take an examination or go on a trip. It takes time to cast a hexagram with the stalks, and the whole process is approached reverently and slowly, like a religious ritual. So it is that one has time to meditate, to think more deeply about the implications of decisions, to project one's feelings out onto the hexagrams and then read them back in a more ordered way.

The hexagrams were believed not only to capture the structure of the present moment, but its potential for the future. Properly understood, the lines are always moving, just like life, slowly changing into their opposites, then back again. So it is that the collection of commentaries on the lines came to be called the **Yi-jing** (*I-ching*), "the Classic of Change," a book that developed layer after layer of explanations over hundreds of years. The result is a handbook of wisdom and personal guidance that has inspired generations of Chinese, and is now used by many in the West as well.

We have noted that divination is really a form of ritual, an attempt to deal with the unseen forces that influence our lives. Another special type of ritual is exorcism, the use of dramatic words and gestures to drive out demons believed to be causing problems. In China exorcism was carried out chiefly by spirit-mediums and Daoist priests, both in the name of gods with whom they had special relationships. We have seen in Chapter II that gods represent order and demons disorder, so exorcism consisted essentially of the priest asking for an order from the gods, which he in turn communicated to the demons, commanding them to leave. The commands could be oral, written, or both. Spirit-mediums in a state of possession by a god sometimes cut themselves and wrote with the divine blood to give more power to their orders or charms. Demons are manifestations of *yin* force, which can be driven away by symbols of *yang*, such as the blood of a cock, firecrackers, swords, and mirrors. Reciting books of scripture and philosophy also helps, because such books describe the moral order of the world, which demons cannot tolerate. In other words, the structure of Chinese exorcism is very similar to the Christian variety in which demons are supposed to be driven away by the power of God invoked by a priest, who is armed with Bible and cross.

Here is an example of an exorcism ritual used by a Daoist priest in Taiwan to cure a sick child:

> Having put mother and child at ease with the gentle ringing of the handbell and the quiet chanting of purificatory incantations, the Daoist next summons the spirits at his command, namely the exorcistic Pole Star spirits, the local Cheng Huang deity, the spirit of the soil, the virgin goddess Ma-zu, and the patron of Lu Shan, Chen Nai Ma. On a piece of yellow paper he draws a *fu* talisman (the model for which can be bought in book-shops) and signs it with a special talismanic seal at the bottom. The Daoist then lights a candle at the altar and recites an exorcistic mantra, or conjuration, such as the following:

> > I command the source of all pains in the body—
> > Muscle pains, headaches, eye sores, mouth sores
> > Aching hand and aching feet
> > [insert the particular ailment of the child]—With the use of this magic of mine,
> > Here before this Daoist altar,
> > May all demons be bound and captured,
> > May they be cast back into Hell's depths.
> > You are sent back to your source!
> > Quickly, quickly obey my command!

> He then casts the divination blocks, i.e., two crescent-shaped pieces of bamboo with one side rounded and one side flat. The flat sides down (*yin* in ascendancy) is a negative answer. The flat sides up

(*yang* in ascendancy) means "the gods are laughing." One flat side and one round side up (*yin* and *yang* in balance) is an affirmative response, an indication that the proper spirit has been exorcised. Once an affirmative answer has been received, the talisman is burned, and a few of the ashes are mixed in a glass of boiled water. A teaspoon of the water is given the child as an exorcistic cure. The Daoist then recommends aspirin, antibiotics, or whatever Chinese herbal medicine he judges an appropriate remedy for the natural cause of the illness.[12]

All the exorcism themes we have mentioned are included in this description, in addition to the use of medicine to cure the natural causes of the illness. So the exorcist functions as priest, psychologist, and doctor all at once, a convincing package for those who still believe the old Chinese view of the world.

Divination and exorcism are dramatic expressions of the Chinese understanding of life as an arena where human beings constantly interact with cosmic forces. In some form such activities are practiced by most religions, and are rooted in psychological impulses still present in modern society. Science has lessened many of the uncertainties of life, but in a way science is an expression of an old religious urge to anticipate and control events by dealing with their causes. The many recent movies about demons and exorcism remind us of how fascinating they can be even to those who do not literally believe, and, of course, some religious people still take such things quite seriously. Our world is in a period of transition, and for many people old and new ways of thinking co-exist. Whatever our beliefs, when something goes wrong we still tend to look for someone or something to blame. It is easier to accept problems if we believe they come from outside, particularly if we think they are caused by another person, group, or nation. The next step is accusations, prejudice, or even attack. So the spirit of exorcism still lives among us.

Meditation

Another important characteristic of Chinese religions is meditation, quiet contemplation by individuals of the gods, Buddhas, or their own inner nature. All Chinese religions assume that self-development depends basically on individual effort, though figures such as

Amitabha provide important aid as well. Meditation provides a method for this development, and accompanies scripture study and group rituals. The assumption of meditation is that by training and concentrating the mind one can attain a new level of consciousness and become a different kind of person. For Daoist priests this means a new awareness of cosmic power within one's own body, power to be shared with a community through ritual movements and chants. For Buddhists, meditation is a means of calming the mind and controlling the ego, so that one can see things as they really are and find peace in a new level of acceptance. Confucians contemplate life's patterns of order (*li*) to strengthen their sense of dedication to the moral order of society. Popular sectarians meditate on the Eternal Mother in her paradise to purify their conduct and go to heaven at death. Daoists, Confucians, and sectarians may all sit in quiet rooms on low stools; Buddhists sit cross-legged on floor mats or low platforms. Meditation can be done either alone or with a small group of other people.

Christian monks and nuns have been meditating for centuries, as have Jewish and Islamic mystics. Meditation has long been practiced as well in Hinduism. In native American cultures, young men went off to lonely hillsides to seek a vision that would indicate their adult name and role in the tribe. The earliest meditators may have been shamans calling down the gods to give them new knowledge and power. These parallels remind us again that Chinese religious practices are part of the world history of religions, a history that includes our own traditions as well.

In China it is the Chan (Zen) Buddhists who place the most emphasis on meditation. Chan meditation is focused on emptying the mind of all ego-centered thoughts in a context of group support. Monks usually meditate side by side on low platforms around a large room in a monastery, watched by a senior monk who makes sure they do not talk or go to sleep. The meditators concentrate on a puzzling statement given to them by an experienced master, such as "Where were you before you were born?" After weeks or months of concentrating on this question, the meditator finally realizes it cannot be answered; that normal logical thought by itself cannot lead to enlightenment. If the meditator keeps trying long enough perhaps he or she will realize that the deepest truths of life and death are not intellectual problems to be solved but facts to be accepted.

The following passage is a description of a Chan meditation session in a Chinese monastery in the 1940s, part of a day that begins at 3:00 A.M. After reciting scriptures and names of Buddhas in morning devotions, the monks have a breakfast of rice and vegetables. They eat in silence, reflecting on the debt they owe those who prepared the food. At 7:00 A.M. they go to the sitting benches:

> In a well-run hall the monk should be able to forget his body and let it be guided like an automaton by the bell and board. He sits erect on the narrow bench, his eyes fixed on a point no further than the third and no nearer than the second row of tiles on the floor. He tries to keep his spine perfectly straight and to control his respiration. Talking is forbidden. The silence must be absolute. If a monk in the east makes a sound, the precentor goes over and beats him then and there with his incense board—and beats him hard. If it is a monk in the west, the blows are administered by the senior instructor present. But the blows may not be struck with the sharp edge of the board, nor is boxing the cheeks allowed, as it is outside the hall.
>
> Those who are new at meditation usually sit cross-legged with only one foot up. Even then it may be so painful that they cannot sleep at night. Some lose courage and flee the monastery. According to one informant, "The pain is cumulative. It hurts until the sweat pours from your body. Some people try to cheat by uncrossing both legs under cover of their gowns, but eventually the precentor will catch them at it and give them a beating. The loss of face is one reason why so many run away." How many? "About 30 percent in the first week or two of each semester."[13]

After meditating for an hour, the monks run slowly around the hall in a circle, and have tea and a snack. Then they resume seated meditation. So the day goes, with seven periods of running and seven of sitting, a total of about nine hours' work, interspersed with meals, short naps, and discussions with the chief monk. The day ends at 10:00 P.M.

Religious meditation is a more concentrated and organized form of something most of us do occasionally: thinking peacefully by ourselves. The occasion for such thinking might be a walk in the woods or a jog on a beach. Our time for ourselves might be while we are sitting on a hillside or swimming to relax after a day's work, but wherever it is, it is a time for new ideas about what we want to be or do. These ideas come because at such times our minds are more open than when we are working or studying. Some Zen Buddhist masters have said that the goal of enlightenment is just such a relaxed and open mind in which we can appreciate life around us in the present, like a child who exclaims about pretty colors and shapes that adults may ignore because they are concentrating on their own work and plans. Perhaps it is no accident that the Confucian philosopher Mencius (fourth century B.C.) praised those who had a "childlike mind," and that Jesus said, "Let the little children come to me, for of such is the kingdom of heaven." So it is that religious activities like meditation that at first may look strange turn out to be based on attitudes and feelings that most people share.

Leadership and Organization

Human groups and activities usually do not last very long unless they have effective organization and leadership, a principle that applies to everything from kids' soccer teams to the United Nations.

North American and European religious groups of all kinds have been very good at organization, as we can easily see from the large number of their churches, schools, hospitals, magazines, and television programs. There have been many organized groups in Chinese religions, too, as has been noted several times already. One organization is that of government officials responsible for performing rituals at court and at officially sponsored temples in towns and villages. Beyond the state religion, the Daoist priesthood is organized as a self-perpetuating professional guild that trains new members in ritual, scripture texts, and hand signs. Some of this material is kept secret within the priesthood. Most Daoist priests marry and live at home, performing rituals in local temples at the invitation of village elders. However, there are some Daoist temples, as well, and a few monasteries.

Buddhist monasteries and nunneries range in size from small temples with two or three resident monks or nuns to large compounds with several buildings in which scores or even hundreds of monks live. There are usually separate buildings for sleeping, eating, meditating, and worship, with rooms for visitors as well. Each monk is assigned a task or office, such as cook, firewood gatherer, treasurer,

Worshipers at a storefront chapel of a popular religious sect, the "Compassion Society."

librarian, or manager of guests. Their life together is directed by a chief monk, or abbot, who is usually a chosen disciple of his predecessor. The monastery grounds are owned by the group as a whole; the monks own only a few personal items like clothing, toothbrush, and books. The abbot usually makes important decisions in consultation with senior monks, who decide such matters as when to hold intensive meditation weeks or a series of lectures on a scripture text, or how to redecorate the main altar.

Temples of popular religion are managed by leading men of the community who are chosen every year by lot. These men solicit funds for renovation projects, hire custodians and attendants, and decide when to have special rituals and pilgrimages, or which touring opera troupe to hire. Smaller temples are single buildings, sometimes with the front side open, with images of the gods on altars along the back wall. More important temples are built as rectangular compounds, with a wall surrounding several buildings. Ideally, the main gate of the compound faces south. As one enters there are niches for guardian deities on each side, then a wide courtyard, in the middle of which is a large, covered platform with altars and images for the chief deities of the temple. Continuous rows of rooms are built along the inside of the compound walls. At the back is another platform for additional altars. Whatever the size of the temple, there is an incense burner in the courtyard on a stand, about three feet high and a foot and a half wide. Here every worshiper places burning sticks of incense and prays to the gods. The incense burner is the holiest place in the temple because it is the key point of communication between worshipers and deities.

Larger sectarian temples in Taiwan are arranged much the same way, and may have been earlier on the China mainland as well, in times when it was safe for them to operate in public. However, the typical sectarian worship center is a small shrine in a storefront or home, with an altar and images at one end of a room. Here people pray and recite scriptures together and sometimes listen to sermons by sect leaders. Sectarian organization can include several levels of offices, from flower arranger to congregation chief, with scripture recitation groups usually composed of women. There is a job for just about everybody, to keep people interested. Some sects in contemporary Taiwan use spirit-writing; that is, they believe the gods can come down, take possession of a writing implement, and write Chinese characters on paper or a tray of sand. Such a possessed implement can be called a "phoenix," or "flying phoenix" after a divine bird in Chinese mythology. A list of officers for such a group can include such titles as, General Supervisor, Hall Chairman, Good Works Manager, Manager for Guests, Service Men, Phoenix Affairs Manager (in charge of spirit-writing), Chief Wielder, Chief Copyist, Assistant Copyists, Music Director, Scripture Manager, Cantors, Master of Rites, Fruit Bearers, Mistresses of Incense, and Bellringers and Drumbeaters.[14]

From this list we can see that Chinese sects are organized in ways similar to Christian and Jewish congregations in North America and Europe, where there are also many organized tasks and positions to provide a sense of belonging and keep the group going.

Ethical Teachings

All religions have some principles of proper behavior, even if these principles differ from culture to culture. Judaism and Christianity teach their followers to act in love, honesty, and justice. The ethical teachings of Chinese religions are quite similar. Confucian ethics are based on love and respect within the family; young people are supposed to obey their parents, and parents to care for their children. Once this foundation is established, one is to respect social superiors, such as teachers and officials, be loyal to friends and kind to people in need. In all situations one should be polite and dignified, basically honest, but not to the point of rudeness. Confucius taught his followers to constantly examine and correct their own conduct, to make sure they had been diligent as students or fair as administrators. They were to seek out friends who were good people and learn from them. To Confucius, religious rituals did not mean much if one was not an ethical person to begin with.

The basic ethical value of the *Lao-zi* and *Chuang-zi* books is noninterference: letting things follow their natural course, without trying to "improve" them. The ethics of Daoist religion are quite similar to Confucianism and also stress that those who seek immortality or act as priests need to be pure themselves. Buddhism brought in some new principles because of its emphasis on compassion for all living creatures, including animals. According to the law of *karma*, every action brings its own appropriate reward, so it is obviously important for people to act in good ways. Buddhism stresses that giving support to monks and nuns is good karma, as is providing food and medical care for the poor and distributing scriptures free of charge. In this way people can be honored now and have a better rebirth the next time around.

In general, Chinese ethical teachings are pragmatic, conservative, and patriotic. They teach that good acts will eventually be rewarded, that people should be content in their social position and support the government. Here are lists of standard ethical instructions from two popular religious texts:

Officials: "bring about good order for all the people; do not covet wealth, or injure others."

The wealthy: "aid the poor," remembering that the "spirits are three feet above your heads."

Scholars: "study industriously; there are rooms of gold in books; don't worry about being poor. If you study with all your might for ten years why fear that your name will not appear on the notice board? [with the names of those who have passed the civil service examinations]. Look at the son of the Yang family who gained great merit and a position at court."

Merchants: "be fair in business transactions, and you will become rich. Just devote yourself to your business; doing good does it no harm."
Young people: "be filial and obedient to your parents. Filial children always obtain a good reward."

Old wives: "if you have children, you must teach them the correct principles of behaviour, and must not allow them to idly roam around."

Young wives: "record in your hearts the 'three obediences' [to father, husband, and son] and the 'four womanly virtues' [right behaviour, proper speech, proper demeanour, proper employment]. Be obedient to your parents and in-laws; you also want to become a mother-in-law. If you husband doesn't act properly, you should urge him [to change his ways]."

Unmarried daughters: "read the *Classic of Female Sages* (*Nü-sheng jing*); obey your parents, study needlework, never go outside to stand in front of the gate. Look at the girl in the story who followed these precepts and married the son of the [wealthy] Yang family."

The licentious: "never reap any good rewards, but just sorely harm their bodies and minds" (here the example is given of an evil man who goes to purgatory).

Those who go out to work in the world (lit., "go out the gate") "to seek wealth, profit and fame; they just bring calamity on themselves."

The specific moral acts that bring rewards are conveniently listed on the first page of another book. They are to

—print morality books to exhort the multitudes
—collect paper with writing on it
—respect the five grains
—repair bridges and roads
—provide vegetarian food for Buddhist monks
—repair temples
—give money to the poor
—buy and release living creatures in the spring
—provide cold tea for travellers in the summer
—provide aid for orphan souls in the autumn
—give wadded clothing in the winter, thus forming good *karma*
—maintain a vegetarian diet and diligently recite the Buddha's name
—concentrate with one's whole mind on attaining Buddhahood or immortality[15]

From this material, again, we can see that Chinese religions are in many ways like our own. Most Chinese people have been taught ethical principles like these for hundreds of years.

Some Related Cultural Activities

Many non-Chinese first learn something of Chinese culture through food, martial arts, landscape paintings, or acupuncture, all of which are indirectly related to Chinese religions through the interrelated world view they share. We have already seen that food was the main form of offering to the gods and ancestors; sacrifice was really a shared meal. In addition, foods were understood to be related to the five powers: sour tastes with wood, bitter with fire, sweet with earth, and so forth. The ideal meal is a blend of these flavors, with peppery dishes balancing the more bland, fish alternating with poultry, vegetables and pork. The typical Chinese dish does not consist of chunks of meat and vegetables on separate plates, but small pieces of several ingredients, each contributing to a harmonious taste.

The physical movements known as *tai-ji quan* (*t'ai-chi ch'üan*) or *gong-fu* (*kung-fu*), originated as exercises to help vital energy (qi) flow freely through the body, and to concentrate it where it is needed to heal an infection or strike a blow. It is interesting that many tai-ji movements are named after those of animals they resemble, because there are references from the fourth century B.C. to people who imitated the movements of long-lived animals in order to seek longevity for themselves. However, tai-ji as we know it developed much later, so the connection is not clear. In any case, tai-ji is based on the same concern for harmony and balance that informs much of Chinese religion, so it is no accident that there are many references to Buddhist monks and Daoist priests practicing such exercises, and to sectarian leaders who also taught martial arts. It was assumed that religion involved the whole person; that real piety should lead to good physical health, that the body was the place where gods could descend and enlightenment be realized.

Acupuncture and herbal medicine are direct expressions of the Chinese world view, for all the organs of the body are correlated with the five powers and yin and yang. Health is the balance of these forces; illness reflects their imbalance. For example, the kidneys are associated with the power of water, so an infection of the kidneys can mean too much water. Since earth overcomes water in the five-power cycle, the cure is to stimulate an organ associated with earth, such as the heart. This can be done with acupuncture needles because it is believed that all the bodily organs are connected to each other and to points on the skin by conducting lines. So, a needle inserted at the proper spot can activate the earth power neded to cure the kidneys. Herbal drugs are believed to operate the same way, by restoring lost balance and harmony to the body. So it is that traditional Chinese medicine and religion operated side by side, based on the same understanding of how things are.

In landscape painting too, the key is balance between mountains, sky, and water, with human beings, plants and animals integrated in the whole. Mountains are yang, water is yin; one could say that such paintings are the Chinese world view in art; their organizational principles are similar to those of feng-shui. Painting is considered a form of meditation, with the vital energy of the artist attuned to that of the scene. In effect, then, activities such as eating, painting, and exercising are alternate expressions of the same understanding of life that motivates Chinese religions. They remind us of the intimate relationships between religion and culture, and of the need to keep a definition of religion broad and flexible.

■

CHAPTER IV

Dynamics: Chinese Religions Lived and Practiced

To understand what a religion means to those who follow it we need to study both its beliefs and how people carry them out. We have already looked at some examples of the actual practice of Chinese religions; in this chapter we will look at a few more in greater detail, drawing from the work of modern observers and anthropologists. The first example describes a family trip to a mountain graveyard to clean the graves of ancestors and offer food and incense to them as a sign of respect. This is done as part of the annual Spring Festival (Qing-ming) in early April, a festival expressing the Chinese world view through reunion of the living and the dead, as discussed in Chapter III. The second account is of the enlightenment experience of a young Buddhist monk, who finds a spiritual peace he never knew before. The third example is of a village exorcism ritual to drive away frustrated ghosts believed to have drowned a young boy, and the fourth, the story of a young woman who becomes a spirit-writer for a popular religious sect in Taiwan. In spirit-writing the gods are believed to descend into a pen or stick and write moral instructions for their worshipers.

These illustrations were chosen because they represent important forms of Chinese religious activity and because detailed descriptions of them are available in English. In its own way, each demonstrates the interrelated world view that is the basic theme of Chinese religion. The Spring Festival is based on a sense of close relationship between the living and the dead in families, which include both ancestors and descendants. Ancestors are worshiped because memories of them strengthen the family and give it a greater sense of continuity and permanence. It is in everybody's interest to participate, because they know that when they die they will be treated in the same way; their influence will continue.

In his enlightenment experience, the young Buddhist monk personally realizes the Chinese world view. He believes he is in communion with the spirit of his dead friend, who tells him, "I am one with you and with all living beings." The monk comes to understand the basic unity behind all apparent opposites. As he says, "I can perceive the latent beauty behind all that is ugly, and the ugliness which lies behind the beautiful. Winter and summer, youth and old age, sickness and health, activity and passivity—all these are but names we give to aspects of the one, eternal truth."

The exorcism ritual is very different from the calm insight of a Buddhist monk, but it is based on the same basic sense of the world as a living system. Harmful ghosts are spirits that have not been properly cared for by their descendants. Since it is assumed that they are connected both to living persons and to the gods, these spirits can communicate their discomfort, and offerings can be made to them to calm them down. If such offerings fail to solve the problem, more drastic means can be used, such as asking a spirit-medium to be possessed by a god who can identify the unruly spirit and order it to cease, desist, and go away. Since, in the system, a ghost is less powerful than a god (has, in fact, very low status), it eventually has no choice but to obey the commands of its superior, the god. So, what may look strange at first makes sense in the traditional Chinese perspective.

The same can be said for the spirit-writing practiced by the young woman discussed at the end of this chapter. The spirits who write are those of dead human beings who have been venerated for so long that now they are considered gods. They still have consciousness and are concerned about what is going on in the world of the living. As gods, they are responsible for morality, social order, and healing, so in their messages they exhort people to do good, give wise advice about how to solve disputes, and reveal prescriptions for medicines. The gods used to be people, and good people may be promoted to gods after death; so gods and people understand each other, and it is only natural for them to communicate.

Now let us go back to the spring family picnic at the grave, a time of more joy than sadness, when the family comes together and there is plenty to eat out in the fresh air.

The Spring Festival

The Spring Festival trip to a family graveyard is described by an anthropologist who went along. A group of eighteen relatives walked about six miles from their hometown to the mountains, accompanied by a pack mule and carrying the food, pans, firewood, and blankets they needed for the offering ritual.

> We walked in three groups: the family head, two male clan members, and myself formed one, the three helpers and the mule formed a second, while the ladies formed the last group. . . .
> Upon arrival at the graveyard the family head took out the blankets and spread them in an open space. He, the male clan members, and I sat down on the blankets, while the three helpers and the ladies started to work. The ladies first carefully put the flowers, which they had gathered on the way up, in front of the two main tombs. Each tombstone was covered with a large straw hat, which most of the unmarried girls wore for the occasion. Almost simultaneously the helpers kindled a fire, while the ladies prepared for the cooking. The helpers did the rough work, such as carrying water from a spring and gathering large pieces of firewood. The ladies first made some tea, which the two boys served to the men on the blankets. They then proceeeded to shell the peas, cut up the meat, and wash the vegetables.
> The graveyard was not a big one, but it conformed in every respect to the best of West Town standards. It had three terraces, hacked from the slope of the mountain. On both sides of each terrace were two pine trees, and on both sides of the lowest terrace were two engraved stone pillars marking the front entrance to the graveyard. Below the plot was a heavily wooded slope. Flanking this particular height were two larger mountain ridges, which nearly joined each other, but just failing to do so, left a narrow gap between them. Viewed from the family graveyard, these ridges were like outer walls with the gap serving as a gateway. Through that gateway a person standing in front of any tomb could see part of the lake.

While the ladies cooked and the helpers hacked wood, our group, sufficiently rested, began to visit some other graveyards scattered at various points on the same mountain. At all of them were signs of activity and cooking. Some families had just arrived; others were beginning to eat. We visited one graveyard which occupied several hundred *mu* (one acre equals 6.6 *mu*) of space and in which several hundred individuals were grouped near the tombs of their own lineages. We visited a humble graveyard in which the tombs were mere heaps of earth, by which only a few living members of the family were gathered. We discussed the merits and demerits of the various graveyards. When we came upon a group which was just sitting down for the grand meal of the day, we were offered some wine and food.

Upon our return to the Y. graveyard, the meal was ready to be served. All the dishes prepared, together with warm wine, were neatly arranged before the two main tombs, which were those of the family head's parents. The family head then took some burning incense and wine and made a ceremonial offering, first before one tomb, then before the other. He kowtowed [prostrated himself] nine times before each. As he did so, paper money was burned. The other male members of the gathering followed suit, one by one. As a guest, I made my incense offering according to the custom, but when I offered to kowtow, the family head prevented me from doing so, saying that I did not have to be so polite. When the men had finished, the ladies went through the same procedure. When each person had had a turn, some dishes were taken to the tomb on the lower terrace, which was that of the younger brother of the wife of the family head. There a simpler ritual offering was made, only by the family head, his wife, and all the women.

In the meantime, the young female relative who was pregnant left the group and went to visit a small graveyard about fifty yards away. There were two tombs, both very humbly constructed. One was that of her mother, and the other was that of an aunt. This young relative made some incense offering, sat leaning against the front part of her mother's tomb, and wept deeply for a long while. Later, other female members of the party with great difficulty persuaded her to desist and to leave the tomb.

With all the offerings completed, everyone sat down to the hearty meal. The men sat in one group, the women in another. There was ample wine, meat, deliciously cooked vegetables, and a portable fire pot similar to those used in North China during the winter months. This outdoor meal was thoroughly enjoyed by everyone in the party.

After the meal came tea and pipes. When the two groups felt that time enough had elapsed, the women and the helpers began to clear away the food and wash the dishes. At about three o'clock in the afternoon the party started on a leisurely return to West Town. En route to the graveyard, as well as on the way back, we met hundreds of other travelers on the same mission.[16]

In addition to what is said about the details of this festival, it is interesting to note the peaceful matter-of-factness of it all. This is just something good, normal people do to reaffirm family unity, to be reminded of the continuing contribution of those who have gone before, and simply to enjoy each other's company. Death is accepted as a natural part of life, and as something that is dealt with by the family as a whole, not by isolated individuals.

Buddhist Enlightenment

The central concern of Buddhism has always been personal enlightenment, conversion to a new way of thinking and feeling. Through such an experience, Buddhists hope to become more open and compassionate persons who have spiritual peace within. The following account is of the enlightenment experience of a young monk named Fa-bao who had just been through three years of illness and spiritual uncertainty. Now his best friend, Tang Jin-nung, had died, and he was alone before his friend's portrait on the altar after the funeral. This is what Fa-bao told an English Buddhist named John Blofeld. The "Path" here, of course, refers to Buddhism. "Universal Mind" means the wise and compassionate way the Buddhas see the world, a perspective that can be shared by all beings.

As was discussed earlier, this new, objective way of accepting the world as it really is has always been the basic point in Buddhism. Such acceptance is possible only when one has stopped seeing things in the usual anxious and self-centered way, a way that inevitably judges what helps me as good and what harms me as bad. Such a point of view breaks up experience into all sorts of dichotomies, such as joy and sadness, love and hate, success and failure, life and death. Life becomes a constant struggle to seize the good side of things and avoid the bad. The problem is that there is no end to the struggle; as soon as something good is obtained (like a love relationship, for example), one must start defending it, developing it, and worrying about whether it will change.

Buddhism tries to solve this problem by saying that it originates with the passions and desires of self-centered egos. If we can get beyond these desires, then we can relax and realize that life does not need to be a struggle, just a process that flows. In Fa-bao's story, we read that emotions such as grief and joy are dangerous to one's peace of mind, and that birth and death inevitably go together. One who really understands life and the world realizes that ultimately all things are related to each other and, in the long run, work themselves out in harmonious ways. Realizing this can bring a deep peace of mind that Buddhists call enlightenment.

Of course, a similar sense of the ultimate oneness of things can be found in other mystical traditions, though it may be called God, or Dao, or Brahman (the highest level of reality in Hindu philosophy). In all these traditions, one needs to come to a moment of awakening, of personal realization of how things really are underneath all the surface changes and differences. One who has such an awakening or conversion can become a very different person inside, even though on the outside he or she may look much the same as before. The reason is that one feels as though one has a new self and a new set of goals for life. These goals may be to "do God's will" or "practice Buddhist compassion," but the end result is often a more integrated, peaceful, and loving person. This certainly seems to have happened to Fa-bao. Now let us look at what he said about his experience:

I think I must have spent more than an hour communing with the departed spirit. No one disturbed me, except one of the family who came in silently to renew the candles and incense on the altar and slipped out again without a word. I don't think I can explain this strange communion in words that anyone would understand, but it was as if Tang Jin-nung had taken my hand in his and said to me: "Why should you grieve on my account? Do you not understand anything of what I taught you? Do you not see that excessive grief is as dangerous to your progress along the Path as excessive joy or foolishness? True happiness lies in perfect stillness. Let your mind remain unmoved by joy or sorrow as the mountain remains unmoved by the winds which howl among its peaks. Birth and death are as inevitable as the awakening which takes place after sleep and the sleep which follows wakefulness. Where is there cause for grief in this? Since nothing exists except mind, and as the individuality of each human being is but a delusion which hides his oneness with the Universal mind, the living man at your elbow is no nearer and no further from you than the being who lives at a distance of eight-four thousand universes from you. I have not gone from you, because 'I' was never there. The underlying reality which animated the appearance of my living body has not moved or diminished. On that ultimate plane I am one with you and with all living beings. Thus there is no coming or going, being born or dying, loving or being loved. All these are but empty forms. Why allow yourself to be moved by them? In the silence and the stillness you will find peace and the end of sorrow."

I think [continued Fa-bao] that a lot more entered my mind and I knelt before the portrait of my friend, but all of it can be summed up in the words, "in the silence and the stillness . . ." That night I returned home feeling much lighter of heart than ever before, and from then onwards I have found myself making good progress in the practice of meditation. That, again, is something which I cannot describe; I can only say that my life is full of peace and of that true happiness which is to be distinguished from the empty pleasure of desire fulfilled. In the silence and stillness of my own mind I find the answers to all the riddles of life. I can perceive the latent beauty behind all that is ugly and the ugliness which lies behind the beautiful. Winter and summer, youth and old age, sickness and health, activity and passivity—all these are but the names we give to aspects of the one, eternal Truth. All the sounds in the Universe add up to silence and all movements have their beginning and end in stillness. This was the message of my friend. This is the sum of my own experience and this is the Law expounded for the guidance of posterity by our Original Teacher, Sakyamuni Buddha.[17]

Exorcism of a Harmful Ghost

In Chinese popular religion it is believed that when people die their souls continue to exist, either as ancestral spirits or as ghosts. What makes the difference is whether or not their souls are properly cared for by the living: if they are adults provided with proper funerals they can become ancestors, but if they die violent deaths far from home, or their funerals or graves are neglected, they can become wandering ghosts who frighten or injure people to draw attention to their needs. Similar ideas about ghosts can be found all over the world. In the following account from Taiwan, a child has drowned in a fish pond right after the image of the chief god of the village, King Guo, has been taken away in a religious procession to another town. People think that perhaps in his absence an angry ghost became braver than usual and took out its frustrations on the child. An exorcism ceremony has been arranged, centered on a small chair held by two spirit-mediums. It is believed that gods can descend into these chairs and make them move, or even trace Chinese characters on a table with one of the chair's arms. The presence of the gods drives away the ghost, and in this way order is restored in the village. The following description is by an anthropologist:

> No sooner had King Guo left than a child drowned in the fish-pond in the center of Bao-an, causing no small consternation to all who lived in the village. It seemed strange to me that he should have drowned, for people said that he could swim a little, and the pond is shallow and often used for bathing. One man told me: "He was pulled in by a ghost. Someone died there before, and when someone dies, his ghost often wants to pull a second one after him. . . . A lot of people have died there. I don't know how many." Another speculated that the ghosts to the north had somehow managed to get into the village.
>
> The dead child left behind a malign ghost, which, it was feared, would do untold harm if permitted to remain in the village. Properly it would have been called a "water ghost" . . . , but so dangerous was it that this term could not be spoken. (After my repeated inquiry one man wrote the word for me, but would not speak it.) Instead it was referred to merely as a "bad thing." . . . Such beings appear to have caused alarm on the Fukienese* coast at the end of the last century as well as in modern Taiwan. Groot (1892–1910) writes of them: "The common opinion in that part of China is that those . . . 'water-spectres' mostly are souls of the drowned. Having spent their time in their

---

*Fukien is a province on the southeast China coast, across from Taiwan.

wet abode in the bondage of the water-gods, they may be redeemed from this servitude by substitution, and therefore they lie in ambush for victims to draw into the water and make them take their place. Thus they are a constant lurking danger for people on the waterside, fishers, boatmen, and washer-women."

People in Bao-an were less explicit about the workings of a "bad thing" in the village, but it was clear it ought to be removed. The death took place on July 22 (the fifteenth day of the sixth moon). The twenty-seventh (that is, the twentieth day by the lunar calendar) was chosen as a calendrically appropriate day for the exorcism.

A little past noon two altar tables were placed on the porch of the temple, and the instruments of divination were placed by them so that the gods might provide instructions on how to perform the exorcism. These instruments I have called "divination chairs." . . . [This] is a small chair, with arms and a back, that measures about thirty centimeters from the top of the back to the bottom of the legs. It is held by two bearers, who are said to "support" . . . the chair. The [chair] is used to provide a seat for the divine presence, and the descent of a god into it results in a bouncing motion . . . and sometimes in violent lateral movements as well. In divination the chair traces characters upon a tabletop with one of the protruding arms. . . .

The first god to appear was His Highness Chyr . . . , the patron of the Jang families in the village and a frequent visitor in séances. He advised that people should desist from speaking "bad words" to one another; that is, scolding or arguing. The death had disrupted the "harmony" of the village, and the village people were being instructed not to make matters worse by adding interpersonal disharmony, but to create as harmonious an atmosphere as possible. His second word of advice was that people should keep their children away from the fish-pond and watch them. He himself had business to tend to other than watching village children every minute. All of this was interpreted from the characters traced upon one of the altar tables by the divination chair. The second chair was now possessed by King Guo. He reiterated the same advice offered by His Highness Chyr, and then proceeded with instructions for the exorcism of the water ghost (or rather of the "bad thing"!). The two gods, represented by the divination chairs, would go in person to the pond and drive the "bad thing" from it. The bystanders must be very careful that it not lodge in their bodies, and to this end women and children were not to approach the pond, and those men who chose to do this work were to carry with them one sheet apiece of spirit money* on which His Highness Chyr would write a protecting charm. His Highness now caused the arm of his divination chair to be dipped in ink, and with the ink he made a blot on each of twenty sheets of spirit money laid out on the altar before the chair. The men stuffed these into their pockets and left in a great hurry for the fish-pond, following the two wildly swinging divination chairs, which fairly dragged their wielders along the road.

Upon arrival at the pond the chairs ran madly about the perimeter of the pond, then hurled themselves and their bearers into the water, where they circled the pond several times more swinging up and down into and out of the water to drive out the bad thing. At the same time the onlookers shouted high-pitched shouts, hurled burning firecrackers over the pond, and threw handfuls of sesame seeds into the water. The shouting, the rain of sesame seeds, and the continual and ubiquitous explosions of firecrackers were all calculated to terrify the ghost, and added to this were the chairs of the gods ploughing through the water, hot on the trail of the startled ducks. When the gods climbed out at one bank, they would leap in wildly elsewhere and beat the water with renewed vigor. Had I been the water ghost, I should surely have fled.

The body of the drowned child had been encased in an unpainted wooden box, and in the afternoon of the day on which the exorcism was held it was carried out of the village to the cemetery and buried.[18]

Spirit-Writing: The Religious Vocation of Qiu Su-zhen

Spirit-writing has been popular in China for centuries as a way of obtaining direct communications from gods and spirits. At first it was used to tell fortunes, write verse, predict the results of civil service examinations, or reveal medical prescriptions. Later on, more of the messages were short sermons from the gods to their devotees, exhorting them to be good and be kind to others. By the seventeenth century, collections of these short revelations were being published as books of moral instruction. The spirit-writing tradition is

---

*Spirit money is crudely printed paper money used as an offering to gods and spirits.

still very much alive in Taiwan today, where hundreds of revelation books have been published by religious sects as their scriptural texts. The spirits are believed to descend into a y-shaped stick suspended above an altar and write in a shallow tray of sand.

The story that follows is of a young woman in Taiwan named Qiu Su-zhen who gradually became involved in spirit-writing at a local branch of a religious sect called the Dragon Palace. The name of the branch was the Dragon Well Hall. From this account, we see that participation in the sect gave Su-zhen not only religious assurance but a sense of social worth as well, because now she had the opportunity to write and teach. This was particularly important to her because her father had prevented her from completing her university education, on the grounds that a girl did not need it. This is her story as told to an American anthropologist, David Jordan:

> Qiu Su-zhen was born at the end of World War II. Her father worked as a cart puller, and her family lived in the countryside outside Tainan City, where Su-zhen tended a few family animals. She had two older sisters, as well as one younger sister, and two younger brothers, and she summed up her memory of the period as being one in which there were more mouths to feed than could be managed on the money available.
>
> Su-zhen went to public school and did very well. In her same class was the son of the district head. When the teacher rated Su-zhen first in her class, and above the son of the district head, Su-zhen's father came to the district head's attention, and the two eventually became friends. The family participated in Taiwan's post-war prosperity, and eventually began operating a small general store on the outskirts of the city. Their tiny store was located not far from the site of the Dragon Palace Temple, and when this building was constructed in 1965, members of the Palace would stop by to make small purchases. Sometimes Su-zhen would make deliveries to the temple for her parents, or her mother would take her along to make a delivery, and the two would stop and worship in the Palace before returning home. Su-zhen's mother, probably because the temple was closer than others and therefore more convenient, developed the habit of visiting it more and more often, against the suspicious opposition of Su-zhen's father, who particularly opposed presenting New Year offerings to the Palace. His opposition was softened when he was eventually visited by a dele-

gation of sect members, who persuaded him not only to permit his wife to visit, but even to visit the Palace himself. Years later, he became a member of the group.

Initially, at least, there was probably nothing about the Dragon Well Branch Hall that seemed to make it very different from any other temple in Su-zhen's family's eyes. It was apparently simply the local spot where one could pray and divine, as one could at almost any temple. Her mother took Su-zhen there to inquire about her health when the girl was sick. And her two older sisters went to the Dragon Palace to receive an oracle about when Su-zhen might marry.

What Su-zhen remembered as most unhappy about her childhood was not poverty or hard work; it was her father's attitude toward education. Su-zhen's father, like many older Chinese, did not believe that girls benefitted from education, let alone required it. He did not mind her attending school as a child, and even took pride in her accomplishments. On the other hand he could not see any point in spending good money for additional schooling for her or her sisters beyond what the state required and provided. [As Su-zhen said:]

Everybody valued boys and not girls. That was the old rural society. I went to school on my own. My father said that if I went he would cut off my legs. I went myself. I walked every day. "I'm earning money myself; I'm not spending your money!" [I told him]. . . . My older sisters finished only primary school. He said: "Girls don't go to universities. Your sisters didn't study; why should you?" But still I wanted to go. If they didn't study, that was their business. . . . I used to go to bed very late in those days because it was very late at night [after work] that I could do my lessons. . . .

My brothers wanted to study and so did I. He wanted his sons to study, but not me. He wanted me to give my money to them for school. I didn't want to. He said girls should get married. . . . My brothers got into a private university, but he wouldn't let me go; he said I had to make it into a public school [with higher admission standards] to save money. The more he used to oppose me, the more I wanted to study.

In the end, however, Su-zhen's father prevailed. She did manage to begin in a university, where she studied accounting and statistics. She had completed two years of college and was in her third and last year when the conflict about the suitability of education for women came to a head. Her father had begun to worry that with a college degree she would be unmarriageable. He ordered her to stop her studies, to turn over her money to her brothers, and to come home to be married. Faced with a direct order, she complied.

The man to whom she was promptly affianced was named Huang Jin-chun. His father owned the large plot of land on which the Dragon Palace stood. Suddenly Su-zhen's life became involved with the Dragon Palace in a way far less casual than it had been before. She was not really opposed to this. Even before she married, Su-zhen had begun to feel an attraction to the group and its activities. As she said:

At that time it was not the way it is today. Lots of people did a kind of martial arts [here, a form of ritual exercise]. It seemed very queer to me: how could it be that everybody could do this but I could not? My mother told me to do it, and I tried, but other people could all do it and I could not. When they did it, if, say, their ... stomachs hurt, they would pat their stomachs; wherever it hurt, they would pat themselves there. They really could do this sort of martial arts; it was as though they were practicing shadow boxing.

Were you afraid?

I wasn't afraid; I envied them and wished I could do it too. . . . I brought some classmates, but my classmates weren't at all interested in it.

Her mother had wanted her to learn to chant scriptures as well, but, although she began studying the art, she abandoned it after a time.

As a new bride, Su-zhen had some continuing contact with her father-in-law's group. Her name is among the contributors who helped finance the publication of a book of Dragon Palace revelations in 1968. Shortly, however, children arrived, and her activity was confined to the household. Although she had occasionally helped in the family's small factory, it was a small place, with few employees, and she remembers this period as a lonely one. By 1975 the children were old enough for her to be away from them, and she took to attending once more.

It's strange. It was as though some kind of power was making me interested and making me think about going. If I didn't go

in the evenings, I would go in the daytime. On the first and fifteenth of the lunar months I would take the three children and
burn incense.

With three children, eight, six and three years old, attendance was
still difficult, but there was little family opposition, since her father-
in-law was the chairman of the group. On the 29th day of the second
lunar month (March 29) in 1976, seven months after she began attending regularly, and about a month before Jordan's first interview
with Su-zhen, the chief deity of the sect, the Golden Mother, speaking
through a spirit-writing stick, commanded her to try acting as a spirit-writer.

> *How did you decide you wanted to become a writer?*

I didn't say that I *wanted* to become a writer. I was divinely
appointed to be. At the time I was really afraid, and at the altar
itself my husband and father-in-law both strongly remonstrated
[with the Golden Mother]. But it was the Golden Mother's command and could not be opposed. Whether or not I could succeed
in it was the problem. . . . There is a secret, a spell that is chanted,
which cannot be transmitted [to you], but [even though that
helps] it also takes real determination.

> *How did you feel that evening?*

I was happy and frightened both. I really envied those who
could help people heal illness and change bad to good [i.e., spirit-
writers].

> *How did the others feel about it?*

They all get along really well with me. When they heard I was
to become a writer, they all said the Golden Mother had chosen
well. . . .

And thus was Qiu Su-zhen launched upon her career as "Phoenix
Pencil," spirit-writer of the Dragon Well Branch Hall, a religious
name and status she acquired by command of the Golden Mother a
few days later. Taiwan sectarians do not routinely keep track of which
messages are received through which medium; the medium is only
the agent of the revelation, which comes from a god, and it is the god
whose name is carefully recorded.

Su-zhen was indeed well chosen for this role. She was much better
educated than most of the members, and she also had an interest in
the literary pursuits of the group.

[In college] I studied accounting and statistics, but I wasn't at all interested in that. I was more interested in the liberal arts. When I got into the Dragon Well Branch Hall, I saw a stick wielder writing characters that I didn't understand at all [because the text was in Classical Chinese], and I became really enthusiastic. My father-in-law wanted me to "help" [in reading them], but everybody gradually slipped away till I was left alone with it. There was no way to stop. Now I have grown accustomed to it, and I've made a lot of progress.

Su-zhen rapidly became the fastest and most accurate reader in the group, a position which she attained even before the memorable night when she was asked to take command of the instrument itself. When she does not act as a wielder now, she is still the best reader. Often she is able to guess a character from the first couple of strokes, as though she already knew what the pen would have to write, and awaited only the confirmation of it by the writing itself.[19]

In Qiu Su-zhen's story there is much that can be found in the experience of members of other religious groups as well. She first became acquainted with the sect's temple because it was in her hometown near her family's shop; and her mother went there. She was an intelligent person whose love of study and reading had been frustrated by her father's old-fashioned opposition and her early marriage and motherhood. But she never forgot that interest in study, and as her children grew older, she found a new opportunity in the Dragon Well Temple, not only to study, but even to help compose books herself. Furthermore, the members of the congregation supported her and gave her a sense of worth and ability that had been denied to her before. Beyond all this, she had been raised in a village and a family in which most people believed in the power of the gods and accepted the idea that deities are interested in the human world. Su-zhen believed too, and eventually came to feel a special calling from the Golden Mother herself to become a spirit-writer. Her belief and level of activity intensified, and she became an important member of the sect. In one sequence of decisions she thus solved several important life problems: her inferior status as a woman in a male-dominated society, her concern for study and reading, her religious salvation, and her need for a supporting group of friends who could help her feel more useful in society. In fact, religions everywhere tend to succeed when they are able to meet just such a complex set of human needs, when they give people more to live for than they have been able to generate on their own.

It is no accident that the first three examples in this chapter have something to do with death and the dead, because death is a central issue for religion. Some sociologists have argued that the real purpose of religious beliefs and rituals is to help people deal with situations beyond normal means of control, such as severe illness, the collapse of a business or marriage, and death. Through their faith, people find comfort in situations that are otherwise inexplicable and unbearable. There is certainly some truth in this interpretation; most of us know people who have turned to religion after going through a particularly difficult time. Nonetheless, there are aspects of religion that this sociological interpretation does not explain, particularly the sense of joy and commitment some religious people have.

In the Chinese cases discussed here there is healthy affirmation of life in the face of death, particularly in the enlightenment of the young monk and the peaceful family picnic around the graves of the ancestors at the Spring Festival. In all these accounts there is a sense of close connection between the living and the dead, a sense of cooperation more than of fear. Chinese religion has provided meaning for every aspect of existence and reminded people that they are not alone, even when they die.

CHAPTER V

Chinese Religions Today

I n the sixteenth and seventeenth centuries Chinese from provinces on the southeast coast began migrating to Taiwan, the Philippines, and Southeast Asia. In the nineteenth century many more migrated after China's ports were forced open by Britain and France. Thousands of Chinese merchants and laborers moved to places like Indonesia, the United States, and Canada. At first they intended just to make some money and then go home, but eventually most stayed and settled down. Despite discrimination against them, the Chinese opened shops and restaurants in many towns and cities all over the world, worked hard, and survived. In cities such as New York, San Francisco, and Vancouver there were enough Chinese to form "Chinatowns," and here they continued many of their old customs and religious practices and established Chinese newspapers, theaters, clubs, and temples. These organizations are still going strong today. In Vancouver, for example, there are three Chinese Buddhist temples, one a beautiful building in a suburb, complete with resident monk. Walking inside it makes one feel one has suddenly returned to Taiwan! There is a spirit-writing sect in Vancouver also, and many Chinese families there continue some form of ancestor worship. The New Year's festival is a colorful time, with feasts, parades, lion dances, and firecrackers.

Taiwan

Since 1950 Taiwan has steadily become more prosperous, and the people have had more freedom of religion than ever before in Chinese history, though a few sects are still prohibited by law, a continuation of imperial prohibitions which began centuries ago. The combination of better education and religious freedom with more leisure time and money has given a big boost to popular religion. There are shrines and temples in every town and neighborhood, many with elaborate and colorful roof decorations, carved pillars, and large images of deities with black or gold faces. The large incense pots in front of the altars smoke with offerings all day; people come and go, praying, throwing divination blocks, seeking their fortunes for the day through shaking numbered sticks out of a bamboo tube. In a side room there may be a spirit-medium shaking in trance, speaking the words of a god in a high falsetto voice, surrounded by devotees who need healing or advice for life's problems. On festival days a Taoist priest might be brought in to perform his powerful rituals, supported by a scripture chanting group, perhaps with a popular opera portraying gods and heroes on a stage outside the temple. If it is the birthday of a god, there will be a big potluck feast of roast pork, vegetables, and steamed pastries, and a parade around the neighborhood with an orchestra and the god's image carried in a fancy sedan chair.

Sectarian temples have all this, plus scripture study and spirit-writing sessions in which new divine revelations are prepared. Sectarian denominations flourish all over Taiwan, some with scores of congregations, all with an active sense that the gods and spirits are nearby, easy to contact, and interested in what people are doing.

There are Buddhist monasteries and nunneries in Taiwan also, some staffed by people who went there from the China mainland after the civil war of 1945–49. In a well-run monastery the monks are awakened at 4:00 A.M. every day by the sound of a huge drum and bell: boom . . . dong, boom . . . dong. They dress, wash their faces, and go to morning devotions before a great golden image of the Buddha, chanting scriptures and the names of Buddhas and bodhisattvas. The monks alternate standing, kneeling on padded stools, and circling the image. After forty-five minutes of worship, they file silently into the dining room for a breakfast of rice gruel, salted vegetables, and tea. After they say grace, one monk takes a few grains of rice and offers them on a stone altar pillar outside the door, for the benefit of all the spirits of heaven and earth. After breakfast, the monks take off their outer robes to devote themselves to the work of the monastery: weeding the garden, painting window frames, sweeping walks, buying vegetables and incense, settling

Buddhist monks at worship.

accounts with rice merchants. Some of the monks may study scriptures in the library, while others show a family a niche inside the monastery pagoda where their grandmother's ashes will be placed after her funeral next week.

After lunch there may be a meditation session or a lecture on a *sutra* (Buddhist scripture text) by a visiting scholar monk. In the evening there is a more elaborate vegetarian meal featuring bean curd (tofu) prepared to look and taste like chicken or fish or pork, plus lots of rice and steaming vegetables. It's delicious. At 7:00 P.M. all return to the main worship hall for evening devotions. By 9:00 P.M. lights are out, and the monks rest until the bell and drum wake them again.

Many families in Taiwan still observe the old festivals; visiting tombs in the spring is still done much as described in the example in the last chapter. Mothers continue to offer incense every day before ancestors' tablets on the family altar, and family members are expected to pay their respects at the community temple. However, since public school education is secular, many young people are neglecting the old ways, particularly in the cities. They prefer to go to movies, ride around in cars or on motorcycles, and chat with friends in coffee shops. To some, religion is just old-fashioned and unscientific, so it can no longer be followed.

In addition to secular education, another force for change in Taiwan religion is Christianity, represented by a large number of missionary groups: Roman Catholics, Presbyterians, Mormons, Pentecostals, and many others. Many of these denominations were active in China until 1949, when missionary work there was forbidden by the new Marxist government under Mao Ze-dong. At that time missionaries from China scattered all over the world, but a large number eventually landed in Taiwan, which, along with Hong Kong, was as close to China as they could get. As a result, there are Christian churches all over the island, along with schools, hospitals, and universities, and lots of free copies of Christian books and tracts in Chinese—radio and television programs, too. It is common now for Chinese in Taiwan to be Christians; to some, Christianity seems like a more modern religion and has the advantage of being associated with Western industry and science. Also, it has become easier for Chinese to become Roman Catholics now that the church has recognized a modified version of ancestor veneration.

There are some Islamic mosques in Taiwan now too, supported by Chinese Muslims who came from the mainland. In fact, the first Islamic worship service I ever attended was in a beautiful new mosque in Taipei, the capital of Taiwan. We knelt on a rug with our shoes off and listened to an *imam* (worship leader) recite the Qu'ran in Arabic. The women were at one side of the sanctuary, separated from the men by a curtain.

The China Mainland

In Taiwan, Chinese and foreign religions are doing well; much the same could be said about Hong Kong. But, of course, the center of Chinese culture is China, and there religion has had a more difficult time, particularly since 1949. For hundreds of years Chinese governments have assumed the right to control, or even suppress, religions they do not like, as we have discussed in the case of Buddhism, Christianity, and popular sects. In the mid-nineteenth century a powerful religious movement appeared called the Taiping tian guo,

"The Heavenly Kingdom of Great Peace and Prosperity." This movement, strongly influenced by Protestant Christianity, became so active that the government sent troops to break up its meetings and arrest its leaders, leading, by 1851, to a vast civil war over all of central China. The Taipings were eventually destroyed in 1864, but before that they had established their own government in areas they controlled. This government carried out a number of revolutionary policies when it could, such as distribution of land to peasants and equality for women in the army. Another of their policies was to attack non-Christian temples and destroy their images in the name of the biblical God who wanted no rivals. The histories of many Confucian, Buddhist, and Taoist temples in China show that they were rebuilt in the 1860s after being destroyed by the Taipings. After the 1911 revolution there were sporadic attacks on temples and churches by radicals who believed that religion had to be done away with to make way for a new China. In addition, many religious buildings were destroyed by warfare, either directly or by being turned into barracks for soldiers.

After the Communist victory in 1949, government pressures on religion became more systematic. Missionaries were expelled, and some church property was turned over to government-run factories, schools, and hospitals. Land owned by monasteries and temples was given to groups of peasants to farm for themselves, and the monks and priests were put to work in the fields like everyone else. People were taught that popular religion was just superstition and was to be replaced by Marxist teachings, better medical care, and modern methods of farming and water control. Many temples or shrines were neglected or pulled down.

However, until 1966, religious activities continued throughout China, protected by the Chinese constitution, which provides both for freedom of religion and for criticism of it. In 1966 China began a new phase called the Great Proletarian Cultural Revolution, an attempt by Mao Ze-dong (Mao Tse-tung) and his followers to start the revolution all over again by getting rid of old customs, ideas, and forms of leadership. Mao stirred up millions of young people to revolt against teachers and bureaucrats, and to attack everything that looked like a remnant of the "bad old days" before the revolution of 1949. All over China people were driven from their jobs, forced to make public confession of their sins against the revolution, exiled to rural villages, or even killed. Many factories, offices, and universities were closed because no one was left to run them. Groups of people roamed about denouncing supposed reactionaries, burning old books, and even destroying antique furniture. Religion, of course, was attacked as well, as an outdated "feudal superstition"; the remaining Christian churches were closed or turned into factories; temples were ransacked and their images destroyed; and all but a handful of ministers, priests, and monks were forced to give up their roles and work at manual labor.

Mao Ze-dong died in 1976, and within a short time the Cultural Revolution ended. But when I studied in China in 1981, its effects on religion were visible everywhere in empty altars, churches used as machine shops, and stone inscriptions in temples laboriously scraped off. Near the end of my stay, I visited a mountain in Hunan province where our family had spent some summers when I was a boy—Nan-yue, the "Southern Peak," one of the five old sacred mountains of China. There have been Taoist temples and Buddhist monasteries on Nan-yue for fifteen hundred years; scores of buildings still remain. Yet when I visited them in 1981, not one image of a deity or Buddha was left, just bare stone altars, a few with fresh incense ashes before them. The monks and priests were all gone, and the buildings abandoned or used as residences by several families each. When I asked what had happened, I was told that most of the destruction had taken place during the Cultural Revolution when groups of young "Red Guards" from the plains below climbed the mountain to wreck every "feudal remnant" they could find. One Chinese hiker told me, "You have no idea of the madness of those days."

During the Cultural Revolution almost all outward expressions of religion disappeared. No rituals were chanted in the monasteries; Christians kept their Bibles hidden under the bed and gathered secretly in little groups in each other's homes. The remaining popular religious sects were closed down, their leaders humiliated, imprisoned, or worse. Scholars no longer dared write about the history of Chinese religions, or if they did, only to ridicule them. Buddhist images all but disappeared from the National Museum of History in Beijing, as if Buddhism in China had never existed. For about a fifth of the human race, traditional religion dropped out of sight, though for a time there was a cult of Mao Ze-dong in which some people revered him almost as a god and spent a lot of time reading and reciting his teachings. But by the mid-1970s that was fading too, and "Mao buttons" and his "Little Red Book" gradually lost popularity.

For a time after Mao's death, his wife and other top leaders ("The Gang of Four") tried to continue his policies, but in 1978 they were removed from power, and China entered another new phase, one of more relaxed and practical programs. Since then, China has been changing rapidly once again; group agriculture is being changed to the old pattern of individual farmers working their own land, leased from the government. Beyond handing in a certain quota to local officials, they can keep the rest of the profits for themselves, and so production has soared. Factory workers are being paid bonuses for better work, and merchants, craftsmen, and physicians are being encouraged to go into business for themselves, once their work quotas for government units have been filled. Scholars are back at work again; the universities are full; and all sorts of foreign companies and specialists are being invited in to help China modernize.

Policies toward religion have been liberalized along with everything else. Hundreds of churches and temples have reopened, and their ministers and priests returned. A few theological seminaries and other religious study centers have started up again, and scholars have resumed writing about religion in any way they like. The government is even paying back rent for religious buildings that were confiscated. There is some evidence as well for the revival of popular religious practices like ancestor worship, funeral rituals, and offerings at temples, though spirit-mediums and sectarian groups are still strictly forbidden. Of course, it is too early to tell how far this liberalization will go, and in any event, religious activities in China today are on a far smaller scale than in the past. The government is still led by Marxists who believe that ultimately the government should control everything. Most people simply do not seem interested in religion anymore; they are concerned about having good jobs and working conditions, modern appliances, and education for their children and about helping develop China's economy. It is possible that contemporary China will be the first major civilization in which religious activities are not of great importance at any level.

Nonetheless, many traditional attitudes that were for centuries reinforced by religion are still powerful in China, attitudes such as respect for the family and for older people, loyalty to the nation, and gratitude that one was born Chinese. Chinese still assume that reciprocity is the basic rule of human relations: that one should do unto others what one would like them to do in return. So people give gifts and invite friends to dinner in restaurants, hoping that eventually their friends will help them out too. A favor given is a favor received; the first records of this principle are from Shang dynasty offerings to the spirits of ancestors in 1400 B.C.! Another ancient tendency that is still alive is that of interpreting human problems in moral terms—as a struggle between good and evil, between public order and private greed—a theme first clearly expressed by Confucius twenty-five hundred years ago. One can see this tendency in 1978 newspaper articles from Beijing concerning the campaign to overthrow Mao Ze-dong's wife and get rid of the last echoes of the Cultural Revolution. In these articles Madame Mao and her supporters are portrayed not just as political opponents but as evil heretics acting only for personal gain. One ditty about them read:

Overthrow the "Gang of Four"
Seize the fiendish devils.

And a headline said,

Utterly drive away the four harmful things.

Some of these terms are the same as those that have been used in exorcism rituals for centuries.

This moralizing tendency is alive in Taiwan as well, as can be seen in 1984 newspaper accounts about a police campaign against organized crime. The chief remedy suggested is increased teaching of morals in the public schools. Consumer protection groups argue that the reason companies make dangerous or unreliable products is that there is too much greed in modern society, greed that can be reduced by more and better teaching. This same approach can be seen in scripture texts from modern popular religious sects; for them, the fundamental illness of society is moral ignorance, which can be cured by preaching and good example.

There is evidence for the continuing influence of other old religious attitudes as well, even if they are not recognized as such. Special human beings are still held up as models for the whole country, either good or bad. The struggle between good and evil is personified; individuals become symbols of larger forces in society, just as were the gods of popular religion. Mao Ze-dong, for example, was long venerated as the savior of China, the bringer of light and hope to all, whereas his rivals were fiercely criticized as evil reactionaries. The Chinese press praises workers who exceed production quotas or invent new machines; they are held up as examples for all to imitate, as are heroes who give their lives to rescue others from drowning or being run over by trains. Virtuous death for the good of all is a common theme in many religions, illustrated in China by the famous deity Guan-gong, a symbol of loyalty and courage. Guan-gong began his career as a valiant general of the third century A.D. who died in battle against the evil rival of a good emperor. Guan-gong is no longer officially venerated in China, but the spirit he represented lives on. In China, as elsewhere, old religious attitudes still have power even for those who have forgotten their origins and may not be religious themselves. From this perspective, studying the history of religions, including our own, helps us better understand the background of today's ideas and feelings.

Some Lessons of Chinese Religions for Today

Chinese religions have many lessons for us today, beginning with loyalty and cooperation within families and a strong sense of being responsible for the order of society. This social concern is the basis for an important form of immortality in China, the immortality of influence, which, in practice, means to act now so that one "leaves behind a fragrance for a hundred generations." Chinese are convinced that what counts in an individual life is its contribution to family and society, through education, hard work, and ethical integrity. Society keeps on going after we die, so by strengthening it our own influence continues; we have not lived for nothing.

This concentration on life in society is related to another Chinese conviction: that it is a rare opportunity to be born a human being. In Buddhist teaching there are six paths or forms of existence, ranging from gods to animals, and demons in purgatory. All living beings rotate throughout these paths, reborn according to their karma, or moral worth. Human life is just one of these options, hard to attain, particularly rebirth in a civilized country like China. Therefore, once we are here we should make the most of it, try to be worthy of our good fortune and live a moral life so that we might be reborn as humans again.

At the highest philosophical level, some Chinese thinkers have taught that humans are to be "the mind of the universe." We are the universe being aware of itself, the only such intelligence we know of. Hence, our role is to think on behalf of everything else that cannot, to complete the development of the world through our culture and moral concern. For Chinese philosophy, humans "form a triad with heaven and earth"; we have an equal part to play, so that without us, nature is unfinished. To use Western language, the human role in evolution is to think, to continue the ancient process of natural development through society, government, economic activity, cultural life, and education; it is these that make up our part of the "triad." This is indeed a profoundly important responsibility; if we do not do it, it will not be done.

Another Chinese contribution is religious egalitarianism: a conviction that the potential for enlightenment is universal, that "the man on the street can become a sage." Confucian philosophers have long taught that we all have the seeds of goodness within us and need only encourage them to grow. They also teach that the real worth of a human being is his or her moral character, something that can be developed by anyone through dedication and hard work. The Daoists believe that cosmic energy and rhythm are present in all of us as the basis of our life, even if we have forgotten it. All we need to do is return to this Dao (Way) within us to find a new sense of peace and harmony with all things. Buddhists proclaim that everyone has the basic ability to understand life in a completely objective and unselfish way. This understanding was first consciously discovered by the Buddha, which means that we all have the capacity to become Buddhas ourselves. For the Chan (Zen) school, such enlightenment is possible right now for everyone who really tries. Thus the three major streams of Chinese religion agree that all of us have the potential to become better persons, psychologically secure, understanding, and compassionate.

There are many other valuable themes one could mention: harmony with the landscape in feng-shui, the Confucian concern for learning as a lifelong process, the conviction that life is fundamentally an arena for moral choices, choices that can change our destiny. This latter conviction in turn is rooted in the belief that in the long run the universe is on the side of order and goodness. If we persist, eventually we or our families will obtain the rewards that are due. As the Confucian philosopher Mencius said in the fourth century B.C., "Those who accord with Heaven will live; those who oppose Heaven will die." Our list could continue, but all these themes are united by the assumption that the world is a living system in which everything depends on everything else. It is this deep sense of mutual dependence and relationship that makes the study of Chinese religions so relevant today. Modern science, economic life, and history teach the same lesson, a lesson we still need to learn.

What might happen to Chinese religions in the future? Of course, no one can be certain, but it seems likely that as modernization continues some forms of Chinese religious activity will keep on going and others become less popular, depending in part on which are perceived still to have personal meaning and a useful role to play. Since death, families, and the changes of the seasons will always be with us, ancestor worship and funeral rituals will continue to be important, as will the New Year and other festivals. There are always some people who want a stronger and more personal sense of religious assurance through joining a group or congregation, so popular religious sects will probably be around for a long time. In modern societies people move around a lot and have to survive as individuals in new places far from their families and hometowns. One way of settling into a new situation is to become part of a group with specific purposes and activities that anyone interested can join, like the Boy Scouts, a school parents' association, a church, or a scuba diving club. Taiwan popular religious sects have the same role for individuals who need a sense of belonging, moral certainty, and a promise of salvation after death. The sects also offer meditation and scripture study, which appeal to those who want more direct personal knowledge of the gods and their teachings. Of course, the mainland Chinese government still opposes religious sects, so they may not reappear there.

Buddhist monasteries have not been strong in China for a long time; the major Buddhist activities of the future will probably be scripture study and meditation sessions for laypeople, along with rituals in honor of the Buddha Amitabha. As with the popular religious sects, the forms of Buddhism that will continue will probably be those that promise the most "power to the people." People want to have control over their own religious destiny, to know what is going on and find assurance for themselves. Chanting Amitabha's name to secure rebirth in his paradise fits right in with this need.

Another form of religion that will probably continue to grow in China and Taiwan in Christianity. Christianity has several advantages, the chief of which is its association with the science and modernity of Europe and North America. Most Chinese want to become more modern themselves, and so if they are inclined toward religion, Christianity might look attractive. The old rejection of Christianity because it is un-Chinese no longer has much force, because China is becoming more westernized, and many of its people have drifted away from their traditional religious practices. This process is reinforced by the fact that the churches in China have been independent of foreign support since 1949 and are therefore no longer accused of representing foreign religion and interests.

In both China and Taiwan, Christianity has been accepted as a legitimate religion for people to join. It offers good organization, seminaries, scripture study, strong ethical teaching, and a promise of salvation. Christian schools and hospitals have long had a strong impact on China and are still active in Taiwan. Furthermore, in China much of the local competition has been eliminated through government suppression of popular religion. If people want a religion with coherent teachings, Christianity is an obvious alternative. In Taiwan the popular sects are very active, but Christianity has prestige, money, high-profile institutions, and trained leaders, due in part to outside support from North American and European churches. Most people in China do not practice any religion at all, but it seems likely that some of those who are still interested will look to Christianity as a way to be religious and modern at the same time. The same is true to some extent for Taiwan as well, though there is more religious competition there, and Christianity still depends on foreign support.

In sum, the kinds of Chinese religion that are most likely to survive are those that deal with basic problems, like death, and those that give meaning to the lives of individuals in modern, changing society. In the long run village temple religion is likely to die out in Taiwan as it already has in China. The gods of village temples have power only over special activities like bringing children, healing disease, or providing rain. Once these activities are taken over by modern hospitals or irrigation dams, the old religious solution loses its importance. The same can be said for the belief in harmful ghosts and in exorcism rituals to drive them away. Children in China and Taiwan are taught that such belief is just superstition, that illness is caused by bacteria, not ghosts, so that exorcism is useless. Therefore, spirit-mediums and Daoist priests will probably gradually lose their influence, and religion will retreat to a more personal and psychological level that is more difficult to disprove.

Of course, the continuing influence of Chinese religions is not limited to China, Taiwan, and Chinese communities overseas, because traditions such as *tai-ji quan* exercises, Zen (Chan) Buddhist meditation, and Chinese medicine are well established in Canada, the United States, and Europe. There are probably more practitioners of the ancient divination text the *Yi-jing* in America than in China; for us, it is new and interesting; for them, it is old stuff. The interrelated world view of Chinese philosophy and religion has been known in the West since the sixteenth century, and new books about it are frequently published. In all this Chinese material some people sense a kind of wholeness and interconnection that is missing in their own beliefs. Chinese medicine, for instance, emphasizes the importance of preventing illness through good diet, exercise, and moderate life habits. When something goes wrong in one part of the body, it is understood to be due to an imbalance in the total system, from liver function to one's family situation and work habits. A persistent sore throat may be treated not only with an antibiotic but with herbal drugs to restore proper blood circulation and with instructions to rest and adopt a more relaxed lifestyle.

Off the coast of California there is a great underwater forest of kelp plants, some of them hundreds of feet long. Like trees on land, the kelp shelters a great variety of animals, all of which co-exist in a delicately balanced ecosystem. Among these animals are great numbers of fish, which have long provided livelihood for California fishermen. Kelp is harvested with big seagoing combines for the gelatine and minerals in its leaves. The chief threat to this life-giving plant is the sea urchin, which likes to eat it. Sea urchins in turn are eaten by sea otters, which thus have a vital role in preserving the kelp forest. Unfortunately, most of the sea otters have been killed by people who want their thick fur. With their natural enemies gone, the sea urchins flourish and eat all the kelp, so that the forests are destroyed, and with them, the livelihood of the fishermen and kelp harvesters. Now, the state of California is paying divers to kill sea urchins with knives and hammers!

In this and many similar instances, we have learned the hard way that all of life is interdependent and disrupting it can bring disaster. This is a lesson reinforced by traditional Chinese religion and philosophy, which remind us that we are a part of the world and need to take responsibility for it. This basic assumption is well stated by the philosopher Wang Yang-ming (1472–1529), who wrote:

> The great man regards Heaven and Earth and the myriad things as one body. He regards the world as one family and the country as one person. As to those who make a cleavage between objects and distinguish between the self and others, they are small men. That the great man can regard Heaven, Earth, and the myriad things as one body is not because he deliberately wants to do so, but because it is natural to the humane nature of his mind that he do so. Forming one body with Heaven, Earth, and the myriad things is not only true of the great man. Even the mind of the small man is no different. Only he himself makes it small. Therefore when he sees a child about to fall into a well, he cannot help a feeling of alarm and commiseration. This shows that his humanity forms one body with the child. It may be objected that the child belongs to the same species. Again, when he observes the pitiful cries and frightened appearance of birds and animals about to be slaughtered, he cannot help feeling an "inability to bear" their suffering. This shows that his humanity forms one body with birds and animals. It may be objected that birds and animals are sentient beings as he is. But when he sees plants broken and destroyed, he cannot help a feeling of pity. This shows that his humanity forms one body with plants. Yet even when he sees tiles and stones shattered and crushed, he cannot help a feeling of regret. This shows that his humanity forms one body with tiles and stones. This means that even the mind of the small man necessarily has the humanity that forms one body with all. Such a mind is rooted in his Heaven-endowed na-

ture, and is naturally intelligent, clear, and not beclouded. For this reason it is called the "clear character."

. . .

To manifest the clear character is to bring about the substance of the state of forming one body with Heaven, Earth, and the myriad things, whereas loving the people is to put into universal operation the function of the state of forming one body. Hence manifesting the clear character consists in loving the people, and loving the people is the way to manifest the clear character. Therefore, only when I love my father, the fathers of others, and the fathers of all men can my humanity really form one body with my father, the fathers of others, and the fathers of all men. When it truly forms one body with them, then the clear character of filial piety will be manifested. Only when I love my brother, the brothers of others, and the brothers of all men can my humanity really form one body with my brother, the brothers of others, and the brothers of all men. When it truly forms one body with them, then the clear character of brotherly respect will be manifested. Everything from ruler, minister, husband, wife, and friends to mountains, rivers, spiritual beings, birds, animals, and plants should be truly loved in order to realize my humanity that forms one body with them, and then my clear character will be completely manifested, and I will really form one body with Heaven, Earth, and the myriad things.[20]

It is views such as these that demonstrate the continuing value of traditional Chinese religion and thought for today.

Notes

1. *The Analects of Confucius*, translated and annotated by Arthur Waley (New York: Vintage Books, n.d.; orig. pub. 1938), pp. 127, 189. The quoted passages are *Analects* 7:22 and 14:37. (*Analects* is an obsolete word meaning selected parts of a book.)

2. *Mo Tzu: Basic Writings*, trans. Burton Watson (New York: Columbia Univ. Press, 1963), p. 88.

3. *The Way of Lao Tzu (Tao-Te Ching)*, trans. with introductory essays, comments, and notes by Wing-tsit Chan (Indianapolis: Bobbs-Merrill, 1963), pp. 144, 160. These passages are from chaps. 25 and 34 of the *Lao-zi* book. Chinese tradition attributes this book to a man called Lao-zi ("Venerable Philosopher"), but in fact we don't know who wrote it.

4. *Hsun Tzu: Basic Writings*, trans. Burton Watson (New York: Columbia Univ. Press, 1963), p. 85.

5. Michael Loewe, *Ways to Paradise: The Chinese Quest for Immortality* (London: George Allen & Unwin, 1979), pp. 98–99.

6. Max Kaltenmark, "The Ideology of the *T'ai-p'ing ching*," in *Facets of Taoism*, ed. Holmes Welch and Anna Seidel (New Haven, Conn.: Yale Univ. Press, 1979), pp. 33–34.

7. *Buddhist Texts Through the Ages*, ed. Edward Conze (New York: Harper & Row, 1964), pp. 202–6.

8. *The Platform Sutra of the Sixth Patriarch, the text of the Tun-huang manuscript with translation, introduction, and notes*, by Philip P. Yampolsky (New York: Columbia Univ. Press, 1967), pp. 142–46.

9. Wing-tsit Chan, ed. and comp., *A Sourcebook in Chinese Philosophy* (Princeton, N.J.: Princeton Univ. Press, 1963), pp. 497, 463.

10. *Folktales of China*, ed. Wolfram Eberhard, foreword by Richard M. Dorson (Chicago: Univ. of Chicago Press, 1965), pp. 79–80.

11. James Legge, *The Notions of the Chinese Concerning Gods and Spirits* (Hong Kong, 1852), p. 28.

12. Michael Saso, "Orthodoxy and Heterodoxy in Taoist Ritual," in Arthur W. Wolf, ed., *Religion and Ritual in Chinese Society* (Stanford, Calif.: Stanford Univ. Press, 1974), pp. 329–330. A Cheng

Huang is the god of a county seat town; Lu Shan is a sacred mountain in Jiangxi (Kiangsi) province; a fu is a paper charm inscribed with written commands to trouble-making demons.

13. Holmes Welch, *The Practice of Chinese Buddhism* (Cambridge: Harvard Univ. Press, 1967), p. 64.

14. David K. Jordan and Daniel L. Overmyer, *The Flying Phoenix: Aspects of Chinese Sectarianism in Taiwan* (Princeton, N.J.: Princeton Univ. Press, 1986), chap. 8. Women can hold all of these positions, which give them more status in a sect than they would usually have outside it.

15. Daniel L. Overmyer, "Values in Chinese Sectarian Literature: Ming and Ch'ing *Pao-chüan*," in *Popular Culture in Late Imperial China: Diversity and Integration*, ed. David Johnson, Andrew J. Nathan, and Evelyn S. Rawski (Berkeley and Los Angeles: Univ. of California Press, 1985), pp. 244–245.

16. Frances L. K. Hsü, *Under the Ancestors' Shadow: Kinship, Personality and Social Mobility in Village China* (Garden City, N.J.: Doubleday, Anchor Books, 1967), pp. 180–83.

17. John Blofeld, *The Jewel in the Lotus* (London: Sedgwick & Jackson, 1948), pp. 82–84.

18. David K. Jordan, *Gods, Ghosts and Ancestors: Folk Religion in a Taiwanese Village* (Berkeley and Los Angeles: Univ. of California Press, 1972), pp. 56–59.

19. Jordan and Overmyer, *The Flying Phoenix*, chap. 8.

20. Chan, *Sourcebook*, pp. 659–61.

Glossary

Amitabha. Buddha of a paradise called the Pure Land of the West. Those who pray to him and call out his name in faith can be reborn there at death.

Ancestors. The spirits of the dead in the male line of the family who have been transformed by funeral and memorial rituals into sources of blessing for descendants.

Bodhisattva. One who has vowed to seek enlightenment and attain Buddhahood by developing wisdom and compassion. Many bodhisattvas who began their quest long ago are the saints and heroes of Buddhism.

Buddha. A person who has attained complete enlightenment through many lifetimes of moral and spiritual development. As a symbol of objectivity, selflessness, and compassion, a Buddha is a model for all. Each world and era has a Buddha; ours is Gautama Siddhartha, who lived in India during the sixth and fifth centuries B.C.

Chan (Zen). A Buddhist school that emphasizes that one can attain enlightenment in this life through meditation. First developed in China in the eighth century A.D.

Confucius. The first Chinese philosopher and teacher (551–479 B.C.), who advocated the moral reform of society through training men to become honest and compassionate government officials.

Dao (Tao). Literally, a road, path or way. In Confucianism the proper way of life for a "superior person," based on the will of Heaven. For Daoism, Dao is the source and order of the universe, formless, yet profoundly effective.

Daoism (Taoism). A priestly or theological religion that developed in China beginning in the second century A.D., with its own rituals, scriptures, and organizations. Emphasizes the revival of life power through contact with cosmic forces in the body of the priest.

Divination. The use of ritual to find out the will of ancestors or gods, through, for example, reading cracks in heated bones, drawing long and short sticks, or throwing moon-shaped blocks on the floor. In all these rituals it is assumed that divine powers influence the process in a mysterious way.

Enlightenment. The goal of Buddhism; to attain a completely objective and egoless understanding of life. Such egolessness is believed to bring about peace of mind and compassion for all beings.

Exorcism. Driving away demons through rituals performed by a spirit-medium or a Daoist priest, who represents the power of the gods.

Feng-shui (Geomancy). The art of locating graves and houses so that they benefit from cosmic forces in the sky and landscape. The best site is on the south face of a hill, above a pond or lake, so that it benefits from the warmth of the sun (yang) and is protected from the cold winds of the north (yin).

Five Powers (Agents). A classification of modes of energy in the universe in an attempt to explain how different forces influence each other. The five are wood, fire, earth, metal, and water; all are forms of qi (ch'i), the one basic substance of which all is made.

Gui (Kuei). Demons or ghosts; usually spirits of the dead who are angry because they died unjustly or their graves have been neglected. Can cause illness, insanity, and other problems.

Jade Emperor. The supreme deity of popular religion, ruler of all the other gods. First became well known in the eleventh century A.D.

Karma. In Buddhism, karma means intentional action and its results, united as cause and effect. Whatever one does, good or ill, is always repaid, either in this life or the next. By such actions we create the form of our lives, present and future.

Lao-zi (Lao-tzu). *(Dao-de jing/Tao-te ching)* The name of a book about how to live gracefully and successfully in accord with the Dao (Tao), the cosmic life force. This book first appeared in about 300 B.C.; its author is unknown, though in Chinese legend it was ascribed to a person named Lao-zi, which means "venerable philosopher."

Ma-zu (Ma-tsu). The goddess of fishermen and sailors, who began her career as a pious girl of the eleventh century A.D. Still popular in Taiwan and Hong Kong.

Meditation. A process of concentrating and calming the mind, usually done while seated in a quiet place. The characteristic Buddhist way of attaining enlightenment.

Mo-zi (Mo-tzu). A philosopher of the fifth century B.C. who taught that people should love and care for each other in practical ways because that is Heaven's will.

Nirvana. A Buddhist term meaning how the world looks to one who has attained enlightenment. It is characterized by nonattachment, acceptance, and peace.

Pure Land. A paradise presided over by a Buddha whose preaching and example make it easier to attain enlightenment. Some Buddhists pray to be reborn in such a paradise at death, which became the basis for a popular form of Buddhist devotion. (See **Amitabha.**)

Qi (Ch'i). The one basic substance and energy of which all is made, from gods to rocks. Differences in things are due to different density, clarity, and form of their qi.

Shang-di (Shang-ti). The "Ruler on High," supreme god of the Shang dynasty at the beginning of Chinese history. Later was equated with Tian and continued to be important in state rituals.

Spirit-Medium. A man or woman whose body can be taken over by a spirit or god during a ritual. In such a possessed state, the person temporarily becomes a god and speaks the god's instructions or uses its power to drive out demons.

Spirit-Writing. Writing on paper or a tray of sand by a spirit or god whose power moves the pen. A popular Chinese way of receiving revelations, moral instructions, and answers to prayers.

Spring Festival (Qing-ming). A festival in early April, a time to celebrate the unity of the living and dead in a family by having a picnic at the grave.

Temple. The residence of a god or gods, who are represented by statues on top of altar platforms. Rectangular compounds, facing south, designed like old Chinese palaces.

Tian (T'ien). Tian, "Heaven," was the supreme god of the early Zhou people, superior to ancestors and other gods. Heaven's approval was necessary for rulers, who could lose it and their position if they were cruel or unjust.

Wang Yang-ming. A Confucian philosopher and official (1472–1529) who taught that the potential for goodness is already in the human mind. This goodness is to be expressed in love for all things.

Xi Wang-mu (Hsi Wang-mu). The "Queen Mother of the West," a powerful goddess in Daoism and popular religion. She presides over a paradise in the west, and promises immortality to those who believe in her.

Xun-zi (Hsün-tzu). A political philospher of the third century B.C. who taught that Heaven (Tian) has no consciousness or will but is just a way of talking about the order of nature.

Yellow Turbans (Way of Great Peace and Prosperity). A popular religious movement that tried to take over China in a military uprising in A.D. 184. A forerunner of Daoism.

Yi-jing (I-ching). An ancient Chinese book of divination and wisdom, based on sixty-four sets of six horizontal lines, broken and unbroken. By counting off short sticks, one can form such a hexagram for oneself, and read in the book what it means.

Yin/Yang. Modes of energy in the universe, symbolized by polarities of night/day, winter/summer, sun/moon. Yang represents heat and light, the power that starts things; yin symbolizes cold and dark, the power that completes them. (See **Five Powers** and **Qi**.)

Zhu Xi (Chu Hsi). A Confucian philosopher (A.D. 1130–1200) who taught that all things are composed of "ordering principles" (li) and "vital substance" (qi). His interpretations of Confucius were made official state teaching.

Selected Reading List

Chan, Wing-tsit, trans. and comp. *A Sourcebook in Chinese Philosophy.* Princeton, N.J.: Princeton Univ. Press, 1963.

Ch'en, Kenneth K. S. *Buddhism in China, A Historical Survey.* Princeton, N.J.: Princeton Univ. Press, 1964.

———. *The Chinese Transformation of Buddhism.* Princeton, N.J.: Princeton Univ. Press, 1973.

Creel, H. G. *Chinese Thought from Confucius to Mao Tse-tung.* New York: New American Library, 1960.

Hsü, Immanuel C. Y. *The Rise of Modern China.* 3d ed. New York: Oxford Univ. Press, 1983.

Hucker, Charles. *China's Imperial Past.* Stanford, Calif.: Stanford Univ. Press, 1975.

Jordan, David K. *Gods, Ghosts and Ancestors: Folk Religion in a Taiwanese Village.* Berkeley and Los Angeles: Univ. of California Press, 1972.

Maspero, Henri. *Taoism and Chinese Religion.* Trans. Frank A. Kierman. Amherst, Mass.: Univ. of Massachusetts Press, 1981.

Overmyer, Daniel L. *Folk Buddhist Religion: Dissenting Sects in Late Traditional China.* Cambridge: Harvard Univ. Press, 1976.

Robinson, Richard H., and Willard L. Johnson. *The Buddhist Religion, A Historical Introduction.* 3d ed. Belmont, Calif.: Wadsworth, 1982.

Smith, D. Howard. *Chinese Religions.* London: Weidenfeld and Nicolson, 1968.

Smith, Richard J. *China's Cultural Heritage: The Ch'ing Dynasty, 1644–1912.* Boulder, Colo.: Westview Press; London: Francis Pinter, 1983.

Thompson, Laurence G. *Chinese Religion, An Introduction.* 3d ed. Belmont, Calif.: Wadsworth, 1979.

———. *Chinese Religion in Western Languages.* Tucson: Univ. of Arizona Press, 1985 (A bibliography).

———. *The Chinese Way in Religion.* Belmont, Calif.: Dickenson, 1973.

Waley, Arthur. *Three Ways of Thought in Ancient China.* New York: Doubleday, 1939.

Wolf, Arthur P., ed. *Religion and Ritual in Chinese Society.* Stanford, Calif.: Stanford Univ. Press, 1974.

Yang, C. K. *Religion in Chinese Society.* Berkeley and Los Angeles: Univ. of California Press, 1961.

Yu, David C., with contributions by Laurence G. Thompson. *Guide to Chinese Religion.* Boston: G. K. Hall & Co., 1985. (Annotated bibliography, by topics).